Stories to Invite Faith-Sharing

Experiencing the Lord
through the Seasons

Written and Illustrated by
Mary McEntee McGill

Resource Publications, Inc.
San Jose, California

Editorial director: Kenneth Guentert
Managing editor: Elizabeth J. Asborno
Copy editor: Anne McLaughlin
Cover design and production: Huey Lee
Cover illustration: Mary McEntee McGill

Reprint Department
Resource Publications, Inc.
160 E. Virginia Street, #290
San Jose, CA 95112-5876

Library of Congress Cataloging in Publication Data
McGill, Mary McEntee, 1948-
    Stories to invite faith-sharing : experiencing the Lord through the
seasons / written and illustrated by Mary McEntee McGill.
        p.   cm.
    Includes indexes.
    ISBN 0-89390-230-6
    1. Meditations. 2. McGill, Mary McEntee, 1948-   . I. Title.
BX2182.M26   1992   92-37
242'.2–dc20

96 95 94 93 | 5 4 3 2

"The Patron Saint I Never Wanted" originally appeared as "Mary on Mary" in **Catechist** magazine (April May 1984).

Contents

Spring   67

Summer   95

A Dedication (of Sorts)

Now that I am moving through "middle age" and working to keep healthy and in shape, I have been trying to walk a couple of miles each day. It's not easy to find walking partners who have a similar schedule and can be there to share the distance, the sweat, and the conversation on a regular basis. Alone, one of the things I have been doing lately to pace my walk is a little personal "litany"—a prayer of thanks for all those people who continue to touch my thoughts and my efforts through memories and through their presence in my daily life. It is to these men, women, and children embraced in my litany that I dedicate this book.

For Jimmy . . . . Thank you, Lord.
For the McEntees . . . . Thank you, Lord.
For the McGills . . . . Thank you, Lord.
For the Dahlquists . . . . Thank you, Lord.
For the Blantons . . . . Thank you, Lord.
For the Schwartz's . . . . Thank you, Lord.
For the Adlers . . . . Thank you, Lord.
For Midge, Valerie, and B.J. . . . . . . Thank you, Lord.
For the Knircks . . . . Thank you, Lord.
For Beej . . . . Thank you, Lord.
For Sue, LeRoy, and Suesmom . . . . . . Thank you, Lord.
For the Campbells . . . . Thank you, Lord.

For the Procaccios . . . . Thank you, Lord.

For Helene . . . . Thank you, Lord.

For the Herrods . . . . Thank you, Lord.

For Lucia and Jim . . . . Thank you, Lord.

For the Sartors . . . . Thank you, Lord.

For Paul . . . . Thank you, Lord.

For Morgan . . . . Thank you, Lord.

For David and Paula . . . . Thank you, Lord.

For St. Mary's Parish . . . . Thank you, Lord.

For the IPL staff and liaisons . . . . Thank you, Lord.

For Seven Dolors Parish . . . . Thank you, Lord.

For the Lay Ministers of the Salina Diocese . . . Thank you, Lord.

For the MAACCD team . . . . Thank you, Lord.

For the Sixsationals . . . . Thank you, Lord.

For the Morning Walkers . . . . Thank you, Lord.

For Bishop Friend
   and the Shreveport Diocesan Staff . . . . . Thank you, Lord.

For those who minister
   in the Diocese of Shreveport . . . . Thank you, Lord.

For all who seek to reveal your Kingdom . . . . Thank you, Lord.

Introduction

We are each on a journey of faith, and we do not travel alone. In God's kindness we have been blest with companions—fellow pilgrims—to walk with us as we move toward holiness, full belief, and the recognition of the realm of God.

Many have learned that one of the things that make journeys easier is the sharing of our tales. We gain energy as we relate the chronicles of our progress, our ups and downs, successes and failures, surprises along the way.

Stories to Invite Faith-Sharing tells the stories of my journey. Often, in the reading and sharing of stories, your own tales are drawn out. The experiences of your heart are made clearer, their meaning more evident. Our reflection and sharing of stories provides us with new encouragement and awareness. Our stories of faith remind us once again that God never leaves us, and we are assured that God is present to us at all times. It is my hope that, through the stories in this book, you are inspired to recall and to share the times you have recognized God's goodness, love, and guidance in the simple acts and experiences of your life and your work.

You will find questions for reflection and discussion at the end of each of the four seasons. These will provide you with points to consider in your personal prayer or in group sharing. The stories and questions can also be used as springboards for centering, for shared reflection, or for prayer in meetings, workshops, or retreats.

I will pray for you as I hope you will pray for me, and may God and all the saints continue to bless us on our journey.

FALL

Ask and it will be given to you;
seek and you will find,
knock and the door will be opened to you.
...Your heavenly Father [will] give good things
to those who ask him.
Matthew 7:7,11

Two Figs

Theme: Gifts of God
Scripture Reflection: Acts 2:42-47

"Deborah!" Yona called. "He is here! The preacher from Nazareth—up on the hill! Come! Let's go see him!"

Deborah looked up from the hot round of bread she had just removed from her oven. She smiled as she wiped the moisture from her forehead with the hem of her apron. "Yona, Yona," she thought. "Such a friend! Always ready for something new, something different."

"Come!" Yona yelled. "Let's go hear the preacher!"

"I suppose I could take a little time to hear this man," Deborah thought. "My bread is done. Daniel will be in the fields all day."

"Give me a moment, Yona," she called. "Let me tell Mama I'm leaving."

Daniel's mother sat on the roof of the house, combing wool in preparation for spinning and weaving. It lay about her feet in big yellow wads.

"Mama," Deborah said quietly, "I am going out for a while—with Yona—to listen to a preacher. The bread is done. There are figs and almonds, too, if I am not back to fix your noon meal."

Daniel's mother looked up, squinting against the mid-morning sun. "You had better take something to eat," she said.

Deborah looked back and nodded. "I will, Mama."

The bread on the shelf was still too warm to cut. Deborah took two figs from a clay bowl and, wrapping them in a cloth, placed them in her pocket.

"Deborah!" Yona hollered. "Come! Let's go!"

"I'm coming right now!" Deborah glanced back at her home: neat, swept, blankets folded and placed on a shelf. Everything was in order. She smiled as she shut the gate and ran to Yona.

The two women walked to the road leading out of town. The day was warm and clear. Deborah felt good being away and free for the morning. Beyond a grove of cedars, a path wound around and up a hill. They could see many people seated in clusters on the hill. From a distance, they looked like the mottled patches of color on a beggar's cloak. At the top of the hill, on a large rock shaded by an olive tree, sat the preacher. He was not a large man but was of stocky build. His hair was dark, and he wore a coat typical of Nazarenes.

Yona and Deborah moved through the crowd, seeking a place to sit that was not too rough or rocky. Finally, they found an open spot of grass not far from the preacher and settled down.

Deborah looked around. Four other people shared the pale green patch of grass. There were two rough men—field workers by appearance—not from her town, Deborah was sure. An elderly woman in a ragged dress sat with a young boy opposite them. Deborah smiled at the child, then turned her attention to the preacher.

For a time he told stories. Some were gentle and brought smiles to the listeners as they reflected upon themselves and their relationships with the people in their lives. Some of the stories confused and frightened Deborah as she felt her heart touched by the challenges of the preacher.

"Be compassionate—as your Father in heaven is compassionate," the preacher told the crowd. "Do not judge, and you will not be judged. Do not condemn, and you will not be condemned. Pardon, and you shall be pardoned. Give, and it shall be given to you. The Father loves you!" the preacher said. "The Father will give you all you need—all you ask for!"

"It would be nice if it were true," thought Deborah.

A woman from the back of the crowd called to the preacher, "I ask for healing, Rabbi!" she cried out. "Will God heal me?" Deborah could see the woman as she attempted to move through the dense crowd toward the preacher. Her appearance was frightening. The woman's head was bent to one side, her right arm hung limp, and she dragged one leg. The clusters of people seemed to move in waves allowing her to pass through the crowd without touching them with her wretched body.

Deborah watched the preacher. Would he flinch? Would he back away?

7

He did not. In fact, he rose, stepped forward, and reached out to put his arm around her to help her. He gently sat her in front of him, and he resumed his place on the rock. His face, filled with compassion, startled Deborah.

He smiled at the woman and, placing his hand on the side of her face, he tilted her head up and said softly, "The Father hears your prayer."

"I know." The woman's eyes widened. "I shall praise God forever!"

"He has freed you of your affliction!" The preacher smiled, and she returned his smile with a brightness Deborah had only seen before in the eyes of little children.

"Thank you," the woman said, and taking his hands in hers, she kissed them. "Thank you!"

He stood and helped her to her feet. She rose. Her back now straight, her head erect, she walked down the hill with the grace of one with royal blood.

A shiver passed down Deborah's spine. She glanced at Yona. Both raised their eyebrows in amazement.

More people—men and women, young and old—came to the preacher for healing. Some were carried or toted on litters. Deborah watched and thought about what the preacher had said, "The Father will give you all you need." Could this be believed?

The day was passing quickly; Deborah could tell both from the movement of the shadows and the grumbling in her stomach that noon was long past.

"Did you bring anything to eat, Yona?" she asked. Yona shook her head vigorously.

Deborah felt the two figs wrapped in her pocket. "Only two," she thought, "Not enough to share with Yona." And, if she took them out, perhaps one of the field workers might take them from her. She folded her hands again in her lap.

The young men sitting around the preacher looked out at the crowd and leaned over to speak to him. "Rabbi," they said, "these people are hungry. If they had food, they would eat. It's time to send them away. They need food."

"Feed them," the preacher responded, looking straight into their eyes. "Feed them."

The young men shrugged their shoulders. "Rabbi, we have nothing to feed them with," one of the group said in frustration.

There was movement in the small circle of people where Deborah sat. The little boy stood up. The old woman grabbed his arm and shook her head at him. He pulled his arm away and walked quickly toward the preacher.

"I have food, Rabbi," he said proudly handing him a cloth bag. "I have food I brought from home." The old woman looked down in anger and embarrassment.

The preacher took the bag from the boy and emptied its contents onto his lap: two salt-dried fish and five small barley loaves. The young men standing around began to grin, but a stern glance from the preacher stopped their laughter.

"Thank you, son," the preacher said, "Thank you."

He then raised, for all to see, the food the boy had given him. He spoke loudly, "Lord our God, King of the Universe, who blesses us with fish from the sea and grain

9

from the field, we thank you for the food you have given us through the hand of this child."

He broke the fishes into pieces and tore the bread into small bits, giving them to the young men and the boy to distribute among the people. Beaming, the boy came back to his group and laid five bits of bread on a cloth in the middle of their circle. The generosity of the boy brought tears of shame to Deborah's eyes. She reached into her pocket, opened her handkerchief, and placed her two figs on the cloth with the bread. Yona looked around sheepishly and offered a small square of cheese to the group. "I thought it would be foolish to share this tiny bit," she said.

The field workers glanced at each other and, smiling, dug into their pouches for small portions of bread and fruit they'd carried that day. The old woman embraced the boy, and they gave thanks for the feast set before them.

The whole crowd was laughing now. Deborah felt a nudge from behind, and a man handed her a full wineskin. A girl came by and offered them dates and more bread. They ate and laughed and rejoiced at the bounty they shared.

"The Father will give you all you need," Deborah thought to herself and smiled.

Finally full, the group looked at all the food still left. "Rabbi, what should we do with this?" people asked. Young men were sent with baskets to gather what was left. Twelve men carried out full baskets to share with the poor of the city.

The sun was setting as the new friends descended the hill. Yona walked with the field workers. Deborah, holding the hand of the boy, walked behind them with the old woman. When they reached the grove of cedars and the main road, they all stopped and hugged each other.

"Maybe another picnic sometime?" one of the men said. They laughed. "I'll bring figs!" Deborah said.

They all hugged again and parted, glancing back and waving occasionally until they could no longer see each other.

"Wasn't it all amazing, Yona?" Deborah said. "I can't believe all that happened!"

"I know," Yona responded, opening her gate and pausing for a moment. "It was a miracle!"

Deborah walked toward her house and puzzled over her friend's statement. "Yes," she concluded, "Surely it was a miracle."

Lord, you have given me simple but special gifts. Help me to be confident enough to share them so that I may help others and in doing so reveal your loving presence.

It's Normal to be Afraid, But Don't Let That Scare You!

Theme: Called to Service
Scripture: Jeremiah 1:4-7

The thought of reaching out to minister to the needs of others is often a frightening one. It was to me.

In 1977 I took a position as a teacher of religion at a Jesuit prep school in northern California. Because this was a boys' school, all faculty members were expected to coach some sport. Lacking any athletic abilities, I was assigned another task. I was to function as a moderator for a social ministry program. My responsibilities included taking small groups of students to visit the residents of a home for the aged. Though the idea of being a wrestling coach did not appeal to me, the thought of taking twelve teenagers to spend time with elderly, infirmed people terrified me! My grandparents had passed away when I was a child. I knew few people over my parent's age, and had never visited a home of this type.

It took all the courage I had to call and set the dates for
our weekly visits. Before our first trip to the home, I
instructed my group to act like gentlemen and to
remember that they reflected the whole student body and
that ministry was part of our call as Christ's followers.
Secretly I prayed that the van wouldn't start or that the
activity director at the home would have forgotten our visit
and planned something else and we'd have to go back to
school. Neither of these prayers was answered.

When we arrived, we were shown around the building,
introduced to a couple of nurses, and told where we could
find things like playing cards and writing paper.

"You're on your own!" the activity director told us as she
walked away.

I thought I'd wait and follow the lead of the boys, but it
seemed that they had the same idea, and we ended up all
standing in a clump at the end of the hall. I knew I had to
do something.

"Let's go visiting!" I said in a cheerful yet unconvincing
voice.

We walked down the wide corridor and peeked into a
room. Knocking lightly on the door frame, I called out,
"Hello, care for some visitors?"

A bright smile greeted us. "Well sure, honey, come on
in and bring those handsome youngsters with you." We
practically filled the room.

Our new friend, Martha, was from Mississippi. She
enchanted us with stories and flattered the boys with her
Southern charm. Two of our group stayed with her. The
rest moved on.

"Go visit Annie in 422," Martha hollered after us.
Annie was a quiet woman with pretty eyes that lit up when
she saw the group. After chatting a few minutes, she asked
if someone would read the letter she had received that day,
and three boys stayed with her.

"Care for a game of Gin Rummy?" a gentleman in a geri-
chair called out. Two boys cheerfully accepted. The rest of
us walked down to the sunroom.

"Introduce yourself to someone here and ask if there's
something you can help him or her with," I instructed the
boys. Within a few minutes, my charges were involved in
conversation, checkers, or a stroll through the building,
pushing a wheelchair.

Alone now, I walked down the hall. A woman in a
yellow robe sat by the window in her room. "I'm a visitor
here," I told her. "Is there anything you'd like to do?" She
nodded and from the pocket of her robe she pulled a small
Bible. "Luke," she said, "I like Luke." "Of course," I said,
and opened to the Gospel written by the Greek
physician-turned-disciple speaking of new healing, new
promise, and life forever.

*Gentle Lord, you call me and I am afraid. Be with me as I step
forward and begin my tasks. Help me to not be stopped by fear—but
encouraged by your love.*

Aunt Lil's Apple Tree

Theme: The Gift of Age
Scripture Reflection: Genesis 1:11,13

When I was a little girl, we lived in Salt Lake City while my father went to college. This was his hometown: the home of his parents, his brothers and sisters, their spouses and their young families. All my aunts and uncles lived in apartments or duplexes—all except Uncle Ed. He was the oldest of Dad's family, and he and his wife, my Aunt Lil, owned a nice brick house on L Street. We spent many Sundays and holidays at Aunt Lil and Uncle Ed's home.

I remember especially a day when we went there so that my father could help them plant an apple tree. I loved apples and, at five, was thrilled by the idea of having fruit available at *any* time. The hole Daddy and Uncle Ed dug was huge, and I couldn't believe it when Aunt Lil carried the tree from the garage. Even sitting on the ground, its roots wrapped in burlap, it was only a few inches taller than me. Its scrawny branches held a few pale green leaves. Two or three fell off as Daddy and Uncle Ed plunked it into the vast hole.

"Where are the apples?" I asked in total dismay.

"Oh, they'll come," Aunt Lil patted me on the head. "We have to let this little tree grow and get strong."

That next fall, there were two or three apples, which my cousin Patrick shot off with his Wild Indian Bow and Arrow Set. The next year, there were probably a dozen. We moved away then for my father's new job in Seattle, but late in the summer we usually visited family in Salt Lake.

As I grew, the apple tree grew. When I was ten, it was homebase for hide-and-seek. We would hide our faces against its narrow trunk, count to one hundred and shout, "Here I come, ready or not!"

At thirteen, my cousin Shannon and I sat on a blanket beneath its full branches and discussed cute boys, terrible teachers, and plans for the coming school year.

I remember sitting on the lawn, my back against its broad base, when I visited the summer after my graduation from college. When my husband, Jim, and I were moving from California to Kansas, we stopped to enjoy Aunt Lil and Uncle Ed and the cool shade of the apple tree.

This last summer, the entire McEntee family gathered in Salt Lake for a big reunion. The reunion was Aunt Lil's idea, and she and I were the planners. We couldn't have been happier as we saw eighty-four nieces, nephews, cousins, grandparents, aunts, uncles, in-laws, and out-laws gather to share memories, photos, and stories. The day after the reunion, we sat on folding chairs in Aunt Lil and

Uncle Ed's backyard once more, basking in our success,
admiring the flowers, and shaded by an old family
friend—a wide, green apple tree.

Trees are good reminders of time and of the continuing
value and beauty of old age. Trees as well as our aging
friends can be strong signs of the Lord's call to all creation
to be things of beauty and of purpose, giving glory to God
at all ages.

*God, help me to be like a tree—sheltering, secure, fruitful—for all
who need to lean on me.*

St. Fred

My husband, Jim, is a gentle and reserved person. He seldom speaks sharply, and you'll never hear any sort of profanity uttered from his lips. Never, that is, until he begins working on household repairs.

If you were to listen in on Jim as he struggled to connect the wires on the VCR or nail down a loose shingle on the roof, you would probably think he'd spent twenty years at sea with the merchant marine.

One Sunday afternoon, I was sitting on the living room sofa, grading papers, and Jim was under the sink in the kitchen, surrounded by wrenches, pliers, screwdrivers, and paper towels. He was attempting to stop a leak.

Each time I was about to make a significant remark on one of my student's papers, I was distracted by a clank or a crash followed by a long stream of four-letter words.

"What's the matter, honey?" I asked.

21

"*Bleep!* I got the wrong *Bleep-ing* wrench for this *Bleep*. I'm never going to be able to fix this *Bleep-ing* drip if I can't find the right *Bleep-ing* tools.

"I'm never going to be able to get these papers done," I thought. Aloud I offered, "Can I go find a wrench for you, Jim?"

"No! It's not the wrench, it's the *Bleep-ing* washers I should have..."

"Maybe we should just call a plumber, Jim."

"We don't need a *Bleep-ing* plumber! All I need is a *Bleep, Bleep...grunt...growl...!*"

I sighed and went back to my papers. I'd assigned my students to study their patron saints and to write a report telling me what they'd learned from their investigation. "I wonder who the patron saint of plumbers is?" I thought. I knew that Joseph was the patron of carpenters and that Cecelia was the patron of musicians, but I sure didn't know who to call on for assistance in plumbing problems. "You never can get a plumber saint when you need one."

I thought for a moment. Actually there are probably many plumber saints up there—probably a good number never get called upon for assistance!

"Oh *Bleep!* What happened to that *Bleep-ing* screwdriver I had here just a minute ago?" Jim bellowed from the kitchen.

"Dear St. Fred, the Plumber," I whispered. (I knew there just had to be a Fred up there who knew *something* about plumbing. I mean this wasn't that big of a job!) "St. Fred, I know that few people call on you for help—outside of your family, your grandchildren and such—but I really could use some help down here! Jim needs your assistance.

I know that you don't know me, but you probably know my mom. She's up there with you. So is Jim's uncle Paul, and my grandpa...," I sighed.

"Hey!" Jim's voice echoed from under the sink. "I think I stopped the leak!"

"Thanks to St. Fred," I called back.

"Huh?" Jim asked as he carried his tools back to the garage.

"I'll tell you later." I smiled and went back to my papers.

When we think of the saints, we usually think of the canonized saints—men and women recognized by the entire church for their exemplary lives and their service to those around them. Sometimes, however, I think it's important to remember that *all* God's people share in the glory of the kingdom. The woman who lived across the street and raised her children, loved her husband, prayed for her sick mother, worked in the PTA, and cried when she read about hunger in the world shares in God's glory in his kingdom. The little boy who who rejoiced over Christmas presents, who wore a towel as a cape to become a super hero, who kissed his mom and dad good night on most nights, and always stopped to pet a dog shares in the glory and the kingdom.

Saints are real people—men and women, young and old—all God's children now sharing in the beauty and the excitement of God's loving presence. We believe as Christians that we too share in that glory and in that sainthood. As followers of Christ, children of God, we too are saints. We proclaim together as we pray the Creed that we believe in the holy catholic church, the communion of the saints, the resurrection of the body, and life everlasting. When we celebrate the communion of saints on All Saints Day each November 1, we celebrate our unity with all the saints: canonized saints, family saints, neighbor saints, and those who live in God's love today. Sainthood is living as a follower of the Lord, and as we seek to do that, we share sainthood.

Thank you, St. Fred, for reminding me of this. By the way, how are you on roofs?

Lord, you have graced us with many strong witnesses of faith and courage. Help me to be a sign of your presence in all I do.

An Extra Chair

Theme: Thanksgiving
Scripture Reflection: James 2:14-17

As a little girl growing up in Salt Lake City in the early fifties, my life seemed ideal. We lived in a tiny, white frame duplex that my dad called "the cracker box." My home was nextdoor to cousins and right behind my grandparents' big brick house. This environment provided me with the wonderful community and security of the extended family. We all seemed to belong to each other. As small children, we never bothered to knock on doors and could comfortably fall asleep in the afternoon on anybody's sofa. Loved, guided, encouraged, and reprimanded by the entire family, we shared a sense of stability I still remember and treasure.

During those years, my favorite place to be was Grandma and Grandpa's house. From our kitchen door we walked only a few steps to reach their back door and enter their massive kitchen.

Grandma's kitchen was the biggest and busiest room in the house. A wide, smooth wooden counter ran down one side. At one end end of the room was a large metal sink with a real water pump, a relic from the days before the house had indoor plumbing. The counter was always covered with wonders—sprouting plants, religious statues, broken dishes waiting to be glued back together, canning jars, miscellaneous cooking items, and an array of flowers, pretty rocks, and feathers brought as little love tokens by the many grandchildren. Paned windows ran the whole wall above the counter. Since Grandma liked light in her kitchen, there were no curtains. Instead, privacy was kept by the many dark green vines that filtered light through new leaves early in the spring and continued to grace the windows until mid-November when the foliage turned yellow to red to brown, finally dropping off, leaving a gray web of tendrils over frosty glass.

A braided rug lay at the door that connected the sitting room and the kitchen. A wide wall held a hutch filled with mixed dishes, vases, and glassware. Beside the hutch sat a number of bird cages. Grandma had one canary named Caruso, and there were always several wild birds in various stages of recovery from different injuries or illnesses. My grandmother was the kind of person to whom people brought birds with broken wings, dogs with mange, and kittens on the verge of starvation. She had a way with animals and was always in the process of nursing two or three back to health.

The centering point of the kitchen was an enormous wooden table surrounded by chairs. On my visits it seemed to me that a few chairs were always occupied by neighbors, salesmen, or family, and that Grandma was always there with coffee and conversation for anyone young or old.

Grandma's kitchen was a welcome place for everyone—and never more welcoming than on Thanksgiving Day.

As a small observer on one of those Thanksgivings, I recall the kitchen filled with continuous activity. From dawn, Grandma, my mother, my aunts, and my older cousins washed, chopped, stirred, kneaded, stuffed, baked, molded, and arranged food for the dinner. My Aunt Peggy ironed two huge Irish linen tablecloths and draped the table with the reverence of a sacristan. The silver candlesticks that sat all year in the chest in the living room were placed on the table beside a large wooden bowl filled with fruit and nuts.

The family began to gather about three o'clock that day. Little ones like me sat two-to-a-chair, close to relatives willing to cut meat and wipe faces as need arose. When everyone was settled, Grandpa stood and began the prayer.

"In the name of the Father..."

There was a knock at the back door. Grandpa stopped, his right hand still on his forehead.

"I'll get it." My dad rose from the table and went out to the porch. Grandpa lowered his hand and sat down. Soon my father was back.

"It's a tramp, Dad. Shall I give him four bits and send him on his way?"

My grandfather was a brakeman for the railroad. We lived only blocks from the train station, and a tramp looking for work or a handout wasn't uncommon. Four bits—fifty cents—would be a generous gift to a man begging.

Grandma looked across the table at Grandpa. After thirty-four years of marriage, word's weren't needed.

"Ask him to come in." Grandpa said, "We have an extra chair."

My cousin and I were quickly lifted off our chair and onto laps. Our small plates slid aside so that a new plate and silverware could be put out for the visitor.

Stepping into the kitchen, the man removed his hat and looked down as if there was some message to be read on the yellow linoleum floor.

Grandma rose. "Would you like to wash up?" she asked as she led him to the sink. "I'll take your coat." The coat was gray and the elbows were frayed away. All the man's clothes were tattered and patched.

At the sink he washed his hands and face, and taking a broken comb from his pocket, he parted and smoothed back his hair.

Grandma stood at the place where I had been sitting. "Here you are," she smiled, "We were just beginning to pray when you knocked." The tramp bowed his head, joining us as we thanked God for the gifts of family and food.

Things seemed a little quiet for a while. Everyone felt uncomfortable with a stranger at the Thanksgiving table. But this ended quickly when my two-year-old brother threw a radish at my cousin Shannon. Everyone started to laugh and to pass dishes around to one another. The food was warm, the stories and conversation joyful, and our visitor stayed with us even for coffee and pie. Finally, as the table was being cleared, he stood and asked my grandfather if there was work he could do to pay for the meal.

"No sir!" Grandpa said firmly. "We had plenty. We're glad you could join us."

"I'd best be going then," the tramp said, turning toward the door.

I hadn't noticed Grandma's absence until I heard her feet on the basement stairs.

"I thought you could use these," she puffed, still out of breath from the climb.

She handed the man a pair of wool trousers, my dad's old blue sweater, Uncle Bill's brown jacket, and a cap she'd knitted last summer.

"Thank you, ma'am! Thank you! God bless you all!" The tramp smiled. Bundling the clothing under his arm, he walked out the back door.

"You should have given him those boots Ed left in the basement, Mom," my dad said.

"Oh! I forgot those." Grandma ran down the basement stairs as my dad lunged out the back door.

Grandma sat with us, the boots on the floor beside her, for quite a while before my dad returned.

"Where is he?" we asked, almost in unison.

"I don't know," my dad shook his head. "I went down the alley and around the block. I couldn't find him anywhere. It was as if he just vanished into thin air."

As we sat beside the fireplace that night, we wondered what happened to the man who shared our dinner—who he was and what it was that brought him to our Thanksgiving table. Later that evening as he tucked me into bed, my father said maybe this man was an angel sent to visit us. Perhaps he was an angel to help us remember the many things for which we are always thankful—for warm kitchens, for food to eat, for family and friends, and for the ability to share the many gifts God gives us.

Help us to be generous, Lord, willing to share what we have with others. And thank you also, Lord, for the angels you send to remind us of your love.

Reflection and Faith-Sharing

The five fall stories relate a recognition of the many gifts God gives us through our lives: our talents and abilities, our experience, age and wisdom, and the gifts of friends and the special relationships we are able to build. This recognition calls us to rejoice in thankfulness and to be open to share our gifts with others.

Two Figs

This story is good for reflecting on the call to service and stewardship.

1. Each of us has unique talents and abilities. Consider for a moment: what are your best gifts?

2. Can you recall a time when you felt a need to share a gift or an ability? Were you afraid? Shy or embarrassed? Bold and eager to share? Reflect on one experience of a call to give something special.

3. How are you called to share what you have with others? What can you offer to the poor, the lonely, the suffering?

4. Are you being called now to use your skill, talent, or ability? What do you need in order to be confident in sharing your gift? Pray about this.

It's Normal to be Afraid,
But Don't Let That Scare You!

*This story is good to reflect on when you stand
before the door of new service or ministry.*

1. Fear and trepidation are characteristic of those called into service. Read about Moses' call in Exodus 3. Read his response in verses 11 and 13 and Jeremiah's response in Jeremiah 1:4-8. Don't forget Mary's response to her call in Luke 1:29,34. If you're afraid or confused, you're in good company.

2. Reflect on your feelings relating to the service for which you are being called.

3. What about courage to make a stand on a social, religious, or political issue? Are you afraid to fully defend what you feel is just and right?

4. What do you need to go beyond your fear? Does fear have to stop you, or can you give of yourself in spite of your panic? Pray about this.

Aunt Lil's Apple Tree

There is a special gift in age and experience.

1. Consider something of great age that you value highly—a tree, a photo, a book, a person. In what ways does age make this person or item more valuable to you?

2. Consider your age. What gifts have your experience, acquired wisdom, and knowledge provided for you? What joys do you relate to aging? What fears? Reflect on this with prayer.

St. Fred

*This story affirms our faith in the call to human unity—our
commitment in faith to be a communion of saints.*

1. Recall a special "saint"—not one of those official saints—but
someone now gone, who touched your life in a special way.
Reflect on the gift, the wisdom, or experience that person shared
with you. "Spend some time" with this person.

An Extra Chair

*Few of us feed tramps at our backdoors. It would be foolish to let
strangers in our homes today, but still we are called to be aware of
our bounty and to be willing to share openly with those in need.*

1. Spend some time thinking back on your Thanksgivings—those
of your childhood and those today.

2. For what are you most thankful? Are there ways you can nurture
and share these things with which you have been blessed?

3. Pray now for those without homes, without sufficient food,
without the love and fellowship of others. Pray deeply and often
for these people. Their numbers continue to increase. Pray about
what you can do—what *we* can do—to end their suffering and to
bring them home.

WINTER

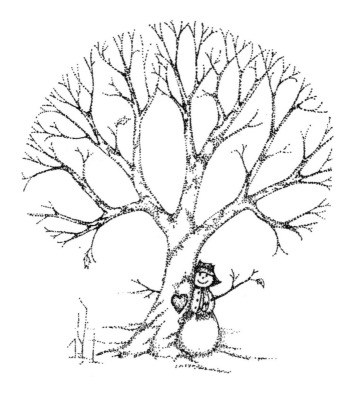

Oh LORD, my heart is not proud, nor are my eyes haughty;
I busy not myself with great things,
nor with things too sublime for me.
Rather, I have stilled and quieted my soul like a weaned child.
Like a weaned child on its mother's lap,
[so is my soul within me].
Psalm 131

Patient People

Theme: Advent
Scripture Reflection: Isaiah 30:15

As a student at the University of Santa Clara and a member of the Women's Sodality, I was expected to go away to a retreat house the week before Christmas. With thirty other girls, I would participate in a four-day *silent* retreat.

"You'd think they could pick a better time of year than the week before Christmas for this!" My friend Liz complained as we drove over the Santa Cruz Mountains to Villa Maria Del Mar retreat house on California's central coast. "I'm tired from school. I'm tired from finals. I'm ready to shop. I'm ready to party! I'm ready to get into the Christmas spirit!!" We both sighed. Sodality was important to us and the retreat was a requirement, but four days of silence was the last thing we needed.

Liz's dented green Volkswagon Bug pulled into the parking lot of the retreat house. Sitting on a cliff looking over the cold, gray Pacific,

37

the cream-colored, two-story wooden building served as a quiet, peaceful place for the reflection and meditation of visitors. A stone statue of Mary graced the front porch. Pink and purple hydrangea banked the front lawn. To the right was a small chapel with the thorny branches of pruned, dormant rose bushes edging the path that linked it to the retreat house. Over us swayed large eucalyptus trees and pines bent by the cold, salty breeze that swept the Pacific coast.

I've always loved beaches, but on this chilly December afternoon the stormy roar of the ocean didn't appeal to me. As Liz and I tugged our suitcases out of her Bug, our complaining continued. Our college basketball team was playing in the Cablecar Classics that week. We would miss it. No TVs. No radios. No Christmas parties. This was destined to be four cold, gray, boring days!

The retreat began with a general orientation given by our Sodality president. Fr. Shanks, our spiritual director, then encouraged us to remain silent, prayerful, and patient throughout the retreat. He told us that we would receive talks based on the Ignatian exercises, be given specific reading for reflection, and would have *plenty* of time for quiet, personal meditation. We were not to talk until the seal of silence was broken by Father.

A dinner of meatloaf, mashed potatoes, and green beans was followed by a talk on God as King and the motivating force in our lives. Fr. Shanks handed out some reading material and by 9:00 P.M. we were in our rooms.

I felt lonely as I leaned on the windowsill of my room and looked at the pitch-black ocean roaring outside. It was too cloudy for stars, and only the lights from beachfront homes illuminated the rugged cliffs along the shore. I wasn't in the mood to read or pray, but I thought that I should do something. Pulling a pen and notebook out of my suitcase, I began a letter,

Dear God,

I'm tired tonight. I'm lonely and unhappy. I really wish I hadn't come on this retreat. I wish I was home, talking with friends, eating Christmas cookies, and resting! But I guess I'm here. You've got me. Help me to see you more clearly in my life.

Love,
Mary

I put on my pajamas, brushed my teeth, and went to bed.
The second day was quiet. We listened, we read, we sat in chapel, we prayed. I continued in my notebook:

Dear God,

You're not helping much! I'm asking for some insight, some awareness of your presence. I don't know why I'm here or what you're asking of me. I think I need a sign or something! How can my life be motivated, directed by you, if I don't know where you are or even who you are?

Love,
Mary

That afternoon I sat on top of a huge rock looking down at the ocean. I was bundled up, but the chilly salt air kept

me in a huddled position. "I wonder how long the ocean
has beat upon this shore?" I thought. "Long before the
retreat house was here. Long before California became a
state. Before the missions were built. Before Columbus
discovered America. Before Jesus was born, or Moses
crossed the Red Sea. Before God made a covenant with
Abraham and his people." I wrote in my notebook:

> Dear Mary,
>
> I've been here longer than the sea has beat upon
> the shore.
>
> Love,
> God

After supper that evening, Fr. Shanks allowed us to talk.
It was mostly complaints. We wanted action. We wanted
answers. We wanted fun. Fr. Shanks reminded us that this
was Advent, a time to be patient. He said that we needed
to continue to pray and that answers would come. The
Sisters brought us popcorn and cocoa, and we went up to
bed in silence.

That night I sat at my windowsill again and looked at
the ocean. The skies were clearing now, and a scattering of
stars reflected on the black water. I wrote in my notebook:

Dear God,

   Thank you for being here. I'm sorry I've not recognized your presence. I guess you've been so near I've missed you. I will try to be more aware of you.

   I still don't know what you want of me, though. If you are my motivator, what are you motivating me to do?

Love,
Mary

P.S. I'm not very patient, but I'll try.

The next morning was glorious. The sun was bright, the ocean clear blue. Seagulls squawked, gliding over the beach. As we waited after breakfast in the retreat house living room for Fr. Shank's arrival, we saw seals swimming close to the rocks. Even in silence we were able to convey an excitement and a joy to one another.

   "God calls us to three things," Fr. Shanks began his talk, "to love, to hope, to faith. In being people bearing these qualities, we give glory to God in everything we do."

   I walked for a long time on the beach. "Creation today sure is giving glory to God," I thought. I wrote in my notebook:

Dear Mary,

Everything I make is beautiful and it's beauty gives me glory.

Love,
God

I continued,

Dear God,

Does that mean me, too?

Love,
Mary

An enormous wave crashed on the beach, soaking me. "Is that a 'Yes'?" I laughed.

That night, my windowsill prayer was different. I was no longer lonely or angry. I truly felt loved, but I still had questions. I wrote:

Dear God,

I'm happy that you love me, but what are you asking of me? Do you want me to be a missionary, a sister, a worker in the soup kitchen? What is it that you want me to do?

Love,
Mary

After morning prayer the next day, I opened my Bible and read from the prophet Micah (6:6,8):

> With what shall I come before the LORD,
> and bow before God most high?...
> You have been told...what is good,
> and what the LORD requires of you:
> Only to do the right and to love goodness,
> and to walk humbly with your God.

Perhaps the silence, the quiet, had allowed me to feel in a more real way God's presence in my life. Maybe that presence could be a truly motivating force in the choices I made and the work that I would do.

As I folded my clothes and packed my bags, I felt sad to leave. There were so many conversations I wanted to have with my new friend. But I knew that could happen at home, too, or at school, or at work. Just before I left for the car, I wrote again:

> Dear God,
>
> Thanks for this special time. I'll try to be more patient as I wait for all you call me to.
>
> Love,
> Mary

I don't remember writing it, but when I got home and looked again at my notebook, under my last insert was written:

Dear Mary,

I love you.

Love,
God

Lord, continue to help me be aware of your presence and your love for me. Assist me as I work to be a patient person.

The Nativity Set

A treasured memory from my childhood is the tradition of setting up our family nativity set. Each year the process was the same. My father would take a large sheet of plywood down from the attic and cover it with butcher paper. Over the butcher paper he would spread an even coat of glue, and then he would sprinkle a layer of sand from our sandbox onto the sticky surface.

"Now we have a desert!" he would loudly announce, as he placed the board on a table in the living room next to the Christmas tree. This was a gathering time for all of us. In a circle we would stand around our new "desert," feeling its rough, gritty texture and anticipating what would come next. Using scissors and tape, my father would cut, twist, and bend colored paper into palm trees, and with peppermint- smelling globs of paste, secure them to the desert floor. Each year the creation of this desert scene began our group effort to prepare the best nativity scene anywhere.

"What do we need now?" Dad asked that year, as Mother carried in a battered cardboard box. "A stable!" we energetically responded. "We need the stable!" Quickly we dove into the box, pulling out a brown wooden structure tangled in tinsel and wrinkled wrapping paper.

We were proud of our sturdy wooden stable. Mother had won it at a Knights of Columbus bingo party the year before. We had dropped it once or twice and Spike, our dog, had chewed on one corner, but it looked like a strong and secure shelter as it sat there shaded by paper palms on the desert floor.

"Who lives in the stable?" Mother asked. "Cows!" John shouted. "Donkeys, too!" I said as we dug into the box again to find farm animals for our scene.

Our nativity set was the durable type—the kind purchased in dime-stores. They were small plastic figures spraypainted in gaudy colors. Each piece was sacred—not by priestly blessing but by the pure and innocent love of little children. They had been sanctified through the years as they were carried about in sticky hands and fuzzy pockets, and made holy by the gentle kisses of little ones. Every year, of course, a few pieces were lost and replacements were purchased to take their place. That year, Mother had bought a new cow. My brother Terry had shoved the old one down the heat register and its ears and feet had melted off. The new cow was quite a bit smaller than our plastic donkey. I remember wondering if it was embarrassed standing next to such a tall donkey as I placed him in the back of the stable.

Now with both cow and donkey in place, Timmy, the youngest, created a bit of a to-do by insisting on including his wind-up bunny with the other animals in the stable. Mother came to our aid, reminding Timmy that bunnies live in the ground and that he would be much happier on the floor, maybe beside the table leg.

"Where do the cow and the donkey find their food?" was our next question. "In a manger!" we shouted, digging once again through the box.

We never did find the manger that year. Perhaps it went down the register with the melted cow. In the absence of a plastic manger, my father made one out of toothpicks and Mother clipped yellow construction paper into bits of straw. It was reverently placed at the feet of the animals.

"We need the sheep now!" Dad hollered. John and Terry had located all eight sheep and loaded them onto their Tonka dumptrucks. They had been "driven" several times around the kitchen and dining room and were quickly *varoomed* back into the living room, dumped, then gently placed on the desert landscape. I put the smallest lamb next to the new cow to make the cow feel bigger.

"And now for some people!" Shepherds soon stood and knelt outside the stable. Wisemen approached the scene from the windowsill. (They would journey closer each day as they traveled from the East.) Mary sat near the manger and Joseph stood at her side, waiting together for the arrival of the Christ Child. (Mother had Baby Jesus up on the bookcase, ready for his Christmas Eve arrival.)

Finally, a single angel with a broken wing and a chipped halo was hung on a length of white thread to hover over the stable.

Now we sat together with none but the lights of the Christmas tree, looking at the scene with awe. It really was not a place of beauty in an artistic sense. Painted figures, broken angels, paper trees—you would never find it copied on the cover of *Better Homes and Gardens*. It was ours, however, constructed with the guiding love of parents and blessed by the gentle hands of children. I don't remember ever seeing a prettier or more sacred nativity scene.

I believe it is important, as we prepare for Christmas each year, that we pass on the traditions of our families and our faith to our children and that we keep in mind the fact that Jesus, our Lord, came for simple, ordinary people. People like us, chipped and broken in many ways. He came to love us and to make us treasured, beautiful, and holy through that love. He invites us to do the same for one another. We are called to mend the breaks and love the chips and to see the value and the unique treasure in each of God's children.

Merry Christmas!

May God bless us this Christmas and in all Christmases to come. Help us always to look for God's loving presence in the gentle, simple, humble, and ordinary things of life.

Best Hound Around

Theme: Treasures
Scripture Reflection: Genesis 1:24-25

I remember the first time I saw him sitting in the dark corner of a small metal cage at the animal shelter in San Jose. He was such a little dog, and he had a worried look on his face.

"Could you take that puppy out?" my husband, Jim, asked. "The one there in the back of the cage. We'd like to look at him."

The attendant unlatched the door and, reaching far to the back, lifted out the small brown puppy and handed it to me.

"It's shivering," I said, "and it's awfully little."

"I think he's just scared," the attendant patted the puppy. "He's only four weeks old—just old enough to be on his own. The mother was hit by a car."

I placed the puppy gently on the floor. He sat and looked at me with that worried look I would come to know well.

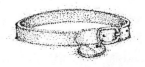

As we drove home, I held him on my lap, petting him and assuring him that everything would be all right, that he didn't have anything to worry about. He shivered and gave me his worried look.

"Is he cold?" Jim asked.

"I don't think so," I responded. "I just think he's worried. He looks like a little brown potato. A cold potato!"

Jim laughed. "That's what we should call him: Tater!" And Tater became his name.

When we got home, Jim cut a cardboard box and I padded it with soft old towels to make a warm dog bed. We put out newspapers and dishes for food and water, then put Tater in the middle of it all. He sat there, not moving, just looking at us with that worried look.

"Do you think that maybe we made a mistake?" Jim asked that evening as we constructed a barrier to keep the puppy in the kitchen while we were asleep. Tater had not cheered up that day. He never got frisky, nor did he attack the rubber ball we'd found for him or chew on the frayed sock I'd pulled out of the rag box. "Do you think he'll always look worried?"

About three in the morning, a pitiful howl came from the kitchen. Jim rolled over in bed and elbowed me. "Your baby's awake," he remarked. I got up, put on my glasses, walked down the hall, and flicked on the kitchen light. There in the middle of the floor was the happiest puppy I'd ever seen. Excited by my response to his howling, he ran to the doorway and attempted to leap the barrier. I picked him up and he licked me and wagged his tail so hard, it was difficult to hold him.

We seldom saw the worried look after that. It only came when the luggage was taken out of the closet, when he got scolded, or when he was lifted onto the examining table at the vet's office. His face always revealed his feeling. You could tell immediately if he was happy, excited, confused, curious, protective, tired, or guilty. All you had to do was look at him!

Though Jim and I were never able to have children, Tater brought children to us. In our neighborhood in San Jose, kids would knock on our door to ask if Tater could come out to play. He was a great ice-breaker and discussion-starter at Confirmation retreats and teen lock-ins. He jogged three miles every day with Jim and still had energy for a long walk with me. He got cards on Valentine's Day and his birthday. On Christmas he got presents from children and friends. During his fourteen years with us, he moved four times to new homes in different cities and different states. He was always the first to make friends with new neighbors. Even when he got old and arthritis and cataracts attacked him, he remained friendly, gentle, happy, and patient.

Finally, however, illnesses attached to his advanced years made eating, walking, or resting difficult. He had that worried look all the time now. As we drove to the vet's, I held him on my lap—all forty pounds of him! He was shivering, as he always did when he was afraid. I petted him and tried to assure him that everything would be okay. I knew it wouldn't.

There was nothing the vet could do. Tater's pain and inability to eat made his death inevitable, and we decided to end his life before his suffering got worse. We filled out a form permitting Tater's euthanasia. The form asked for the animal's name, age, size, and breed. Under breed, Jim wrote, "best hound around."

I think I don't consider enough the unique gifts God gives me. I also fail to consider the brevity of their presence. The death of our pet opened a window for me to see more clearly the wonderful treasures I have—treasure in friends, in the beauty of nature, in energy and good health—in all the things that bring me joy. Tater's death has helped me reflect more closely on the importance of recognizing and being thankful for all God's gifts. It has also made me aware of their (and our) temporary nature—until, of course, we are once more united with God and all the saints and the gifts of God's glory in heaven.

Thank you, Tater, for all you taught us! You were truly the best hound around!

Help me, Lord, Master of all creation, to recognize your beauty in all the wonders of your world.

A Reflection on the Divine Office (for Laity)

Theme: Holy Family
Scripture Reflection: 1 Thessalonians 5:17

At the mid-morning break in a class I was teaching on prayer and reflection, three women stood around the coffee pot and complained.

"I wish I could pray like the sisters and the priests," one of them said. "I'd love to have that peaceful time, set apart just for meditation like religious have. The Divine Office...like that."

"I know what you mean," said another. "I wish bells would ring, calling me to stop everything and remember that God is present in all the action of my day."

"Don't we already do that?" I asked.

They looked at me quizzically.

"Maybe we already have a Divine Office and we just haven't recognized it yet."

"Explain," they said, as we walked back to begin class again.

"I'll have it ready next week if you'll help," I responded. They looked at each other, shrugged their shoulders, and agreed. Here's what we came up with:

> The Divine Office is a traditional prayer of the Church for praising God and for sanctifying the day. It was celebrated daily as a sacred obligation by priests, subdeacons, and men and women who professed solemn vows. Its origin goes back to early Christian times and was developed so that the whole course of the day and night was made holy by recognition of God's presence.
>
> *1968 National Catholic Almanac*

Matins
(First Prayer)

The first call to prayer rang in the dead of night. Religious gathered together to keep vigil for the Lord's coming. In longing, they cried out in prayer: "*Veni, Domine, Jesu!*" "Come, Lord Jesus!"

In the dead of night parents wait for a teenager's return. A father rocks a sick child. A mother nurses an infant. They carry in their hearts the knowledge that in spite of the darkness, an inextinguishable light shines for them. Longing, they cry out in prayer: "*Veni, Domine Jesu!*" "Come, Lord Jesus!"

Lauds
(Laudes Matutinae: Morning Prayer)

In this jubilant hour of freshness and light, all in chapel give resounding praise to the Lord's new day!

Stirring oatmeal, ironing a wrinkled shirt, kissing awake a sleeping spouse. Over yells and laughter the family wakes. All resound the beginning of a new day.

Prime
(The "Little" Hour)

This prayer begins the work of the day—a time for monks to reflect upon their labor in the Lord's vineyard, a time to recall the yoke is easy and the burden light. It is a time to recognize that the Lord is present to guide the toil.

The toddler is delivered to daycare and the children dropped off at school. Now for the ten-minute drive to work. Marie turns off the radio amid freeway traffic to recall God's presence, to pray for confidence and patience through the day, and to thank God for purpose in life.

55

Terse
(Another "Little" Hour)

Just a brief, mid-morning pause for the community to pray: "Come, Holy Spirit, Breath of God."

Over coffee and donuts, workers share a few moments, just a little time to catch a breath. "Come, Holy Spirit, Breath of God."

Sext
(A Noon Prayer)

The community gathers to recognize life at its fullness and to pray to fight off weariness and the temptation to slack as the day continues.

A teacher sits over a tuna sandwich and a Coke—papers to grade and three more classes to go. He prays for energy to complete his day and for openness to his students' thoughts.

None
(A Prayer for Perseverance)

Though weary, the community joins in prayer to make ready for earthly, as well as heavenly, banquets.

Sharon peels carrots. Danny sets the table. Dad checks the meatloaf. A tired family prepares their evening meal—a good time to chat, to share events of the day, to listen and nurture and love.

Vespers
(Evening Prayer)

As the sun sets, the community is called together to give thanks.

A family holds hands around the table. "Bless us, O Lord..." Together, they give thanks, remembering to pray for those of the family unable to be present for the evening meal because of play practice, a meeting, a game.

Compline
(Prayer at Day's End)

Now is the time for personal reflection. The community asks for God's protection through the dangers and darkness of night. In silence, monks return to their cells to pray and sleep.

Together, a couple sits quietly on the sofa. The children—tucked, kissed, and blessed—are sleeping now. Without words, they pray together for God's protective presence in their home. They thank God for this quiet time alone and share a small but truly sacred kiss as Johnny Carson begins his monologue.

Amen! Amen!

Lord, help me to make each moment of my day a prayer!

"Big Ed"

Theme: Witness
Scripture Reflection: Acts 2:46-47

I first met Ed when he called me at my parish office in response to a bulletin notice I had been running that expressed my need for a volunteer religion teacher.

"I hear you want somebody to teach the fifth grade," he said in a strong, deep voice. "Do you take rednecks?"

I had been looking for someone to fill the fifth-grade space for weeks now, but I'd been in the business too long to take just anybody.

"I guess it depends on how red the neck is," I responded. "It's a pretty demanding job. This program involves teaching the children every weekday before their regular school classes begin. That's more than five hours a week." I waited for a negative response.

"I've got the time," he told me.

"Okay," I said, "let's get together and you can tell me about yourself. I'll tell you about the religious education

59

program, go over the text with you, and we'll see if this can work out."

We set a time to meet. That afternoon I put materials together and drove to his house.

He was a big man who had been in construction for many years. He had a wife and grown children, loved to fish, and had deep love for the faith. Though his own religious leanings seemed to be fairly traditional and on the conservative side, he was willing to attend the parish teacher-training courses and work with our modern text series. He hadn't taught before, but he saw the need and was eager to help.

It only took a few days before Ed and his students were fully bonded. The kids affectionately called him Big Ed and seemed to always enjoy his stories, lessons, and his witness of faith. Ed worked hard to teach the lessons in the text and loved to increase his students' understanding of prayer, reflection, the mass, and the importance of the children's full participation in liturgy. Along with opening his heart to his class, he opened his home. They still talk about one rainy October Saturday when they were invited to Ed's to build crooked little grottoes out of small stones and wet cement for the Blessed Mother and how Ed's wife, Mary, fed them hotdogs and potato salad. The fifth graders loved Ed and he loved them.

Early one winter morning, I got a call from Mary. Ed wouldn't be at class. She was calling from the hospital. He had a dangerous blood clot. His condition was serious. It was touch and go. In a shaky voice, Mary asked me to tell the class and to pray for Ed.

I was in the fifth-grade room when the class arrived.

"Big Ed is in the hospital," I told them, trying to explain the situation briefly. "He's very sick. He needs your prayers."

"Could he die, Mrs. McGill?" one of the kids asked. "Is he really, really sick?"

"Really, really sick," I said.

We prayed together and talked quietly. I tried to introduce the day's lesson, but neither my heart nor theirs was really in it. Class ended, and I left as they prepared for their regular school day.

At 3:35 that afternoon, just after the bell rang through the buildings across the street ending the school day, six fifth- graders entered my office, escorted by the parish secretary. "From Big Ed's class." she said and left. Their faces were bright and expressed an excitement only children seem able to emit.

Approaching my desk, a boy with sandy hair and a bright blue, hooded jacket removed his gloves, reached into his pockets, and dropped handfuls of coins and two crumpled dollar bills onto my blotter. "We had a collection, Mrs. McGill. Is this enough to buy a mass for Big Ed?"

Before I could remind them that we don't "buy" masses, one of the girls came around the desk and unfolded a piece of binder paper.

"We prepared the mass during lunch. The teachers let our class stay in the cafeteria and we planned it all." She glowed. "This is the opening song, and Danny will do the first reading. We chose it from Isaiah."

They had three songs, two readings, and special intercessions. All the liturgical roles had been assigned and listed on the sheet of paper—servers, readers, music, leaders, gift bearers.

"Can Father do this tomorrow at eight?" The smallest of the children smiled. "We told all the kids we'd call them tonight! Big Ed needs our prayers!"

I don't know when I've felt prouder of a teacher and a class than right then. I still feel proud telling the story.

Big Ed did recover and return to teach that fifth-grade class and fifth-grade classes in following years. I've also heard that somewhere deep in a bedroom drawer in Big Ed's house is a folded piece of binder paper listing three songs and two readings and the names of special liturgical ministers. And good sources tell me that even today in the homes of some young adults tucked in boxes in attics or sitting on the back of shelves of basement walls are small, crooked cement and stone grottoes for the Blessed Mother. And encouraging many hearts is the memory of a religion teacher who taught not just the text but witnessed the love of God, the mass, and the faith.

Father, help me to be a teacher who stands as a true witness of your love and your presence in all that I do.

Questions for Reflection and Faith-Sharing

Winter's stories lead us to reflect on quiet time, patient waiting, centering, cocooning. In winter we seek simplicity and the joy of sharing time as family and community. In winter's chill we pray for a peaceful time to rest, calm and secure in God's warm arms.

Patient People

This is a story about the difficulty of waiting and taking time to spend in the presence of the Lord.

1. We are people in the "fast lane." We can't waste time! We are in a hurry to get from here to there—wherever that is. *Stop* for a moment. Take a deep breath. Know that God is present.

2. Can you recall a time when rushing or your impatience kept you from enjoying an experience or from recognizing the value of your effort?

3. What can you do to allow yourself a little space, a little time to sit patiently in the presence of the Lord?

4. Try writing a letter to the Lord. Reflect on God's response. Letters to God, or journaling, can be wonderful ways to pray.

The Nativity Set

True beauty and holiness are not determined by perfection or material value. Beauty and holiness are determined in your heart.

1. Think back to the holiday traditions of your youth. What experiences do you recall as truly beautiful—perhaps even holy?

2. Share a Christmas story with a friend, your spouse, a child. Ask that he or she share a story with you. Reflect together on why the story is important and so clear in memory.

3. If we believe that real beauty is in the eye of the beholder or in our memory, what can be said about our feelings and the feelings of society relating to "looking good?" Reflect for a moment on the real beauty you possess.

Best Hound Around

This story reflects on recognition of God's gifts and their temporary nature.

1. Have you had an experience like that in this story? Has a pet touched your life? Consider what you have learned from pets or from creatures you have observed, such as birds or squirrels.

2. We cannot be assured continued possession of our gifts—gifts of good health, property, employment, family, friends, pets, even life. Reflect upon the brevity of God's gifts to you. Does their value lie in your knowledge that all is fleeting? How does it change the way you look upon your possessions and your relationships?

3. God gave us the responsibility of caring for creation: the land and the creatures who live in its forests, mountains, plains, waters, and skies. Pray about this important charge.

A Reflection on the Divine Office (for Laity)

This story offers a modern look at a traditional form of daily prayer.

1. In light of the reflection, what are the times when you exercise your daily prayer?

2. What does it take to make something holy or blessed? What does it take to make an experience a prayer?

"Big Ed"

Here we reflect upon how our daily lives witness our faith.

1. Ed's example—his love for his students and for the liturgy—stirred his class to do the same. When Ed became seriously ill, these children responded with beautiful faith. They used what he had taught them to relate with hope and with prayer to this difficult situation. What examples do you provide for those around you? What traits of strength do you have to offer in the face of hardships?

2. Reflect on how you could better witness your faith and your love for God and for others.

SPRING

Behold,
I make all things new!
Revelation 21:5

The Clothesline

Theme: Linking
Scripture Reflection: Deuteronomy 7:9

I pulled the warm, damp wads of laundry out of the washing machine and tossed them vigorously into the clothes dryer. I set the time and temperature, shut the dryer door, and pushed the button marked "Start."

Nothing happened.

I opened the door, made sure that nothing was blocking its closure, firmly closed it, and again pushed the button.

Nothing happened.

I opened the door once more, carefully adjusted the weight of the load, reset the dial, climbed over the top of the machine and looked over the back to make sure the plug was in its socket, securely shut the door, and pushed the button.

Nothing happened!

"I don't have time for this!" I mumbled to myself. "I have better things to do than deal with a broken clothes dryer!"

I transferred the now clammy wash to a wicker basket
and spent about ten minutes hunting for the box of
clothespins I had stowed away somewhere in one of the
laundry room cupboards. I then maneuvered basket and
clothespins out of the house, through the garage, and into
an overgrown corner of the backyard where an ancient,
sagging clothesline hung.

"This is the pits!" I thought out loud, "The true pits!"

The morning was clear and beginning to warm. Huge
red poppies clustered in patches along the fence. Some
noisy birds chattered in the elm tree. As I began to hang
the first piece of laundry onto the line, an unexpected gust
of wind whipped in and flapped a cold, wet pillowcase into
my face. It was almost like the comic slap in a cartoon or
vaudeville skit. "Snap out of it!" I had to laugh. My
grumpiness dissolved with my laughter, and I began to
hang out my wash, piece by piece.

As I linked towel to placemat to Jim's T-shirt to my
bathrobe, I recalled watching my mother through the small
glass panes of our kitchen door as she hung clothes. She
seemed so tall then, reaching up, clipping diaper to diaper
to T-shirt to bib—my father's long-sleeved white shirts, her
pretty blue apron with the yellow rick-rack, my pink church
dress on which Grandma had embroidered clusters of
flowers.

Now an image of Grandma focused in my mind—
hanging white sheets in the hot South Dakota sun,
Grandpa's dark blue overalls and plaid shirts, the linen
tablecloth her great aunt had given her as a wedding gift

and that she'd used at the party celebrating my mother's
First Communion.

That day, my simple experience of hanging clothes
somehow linked me to the other women in my life and to
the communities and families they had worked to hold
together. As I linked our clothes together, I envisioned
women throughout history exercising this ageless
ritual—briefly, symbolically connecting together their
children, their husbands, the persons under their care and
concern. I could imagine pioneer women hanging
river-washed clothes on the branches of bushes to dry in
the sun. I could see women chatting at city wells in
Medieval Europe as they wrung water from their families'
clothing. I could see Mary, laughing with other women,
pulling the clothes of her husband, Joseph, and their child,
Jesus, down from the limbs of an olive tree, folding them
to carry back home. I could see Sarah rejoicing as she
hung the garments of Abraham next to the small clothes of
their unexpected child, Isaac.

God has blessed women with a special task—the task of
somehow pulling together the people they care for and
calling them into family, a community of love and of
harmony. Because this is a most difficult task, God
provided a wonderful symbol—hanging their hopes before
the wind, the breath of God to bless them, to bring them
new life, to give them renewed purpose.

My basket was empty. My heart was full. "Thank you,
Lord," I whispered, "for revealing your presence so vividly
in this most ordinary of jobs. Thank you for my
womanhood, and thank you for the women who worked

to keep me linked to you and to the family with whom I have been gifted: mothers, teachers, neighbors, friends.

Father/Mother God, help me, in whatever I do, to be one who works to link, to join, to connect, to secure your much-loved family here, revealing in its unity the wonderful presence of your Kingdom.

A Most Persistent Woman

Theme: Answered Prayer
Scripture Reflection: Psalm 91:5,9

Merah pulled the wet cloth from the bowl, wrung it dry,
and placed it gently on her daughter's forehead. The girl
was terribly hot. Her sleep was fitful, and she cried softly.

"If only I could do something to cool her—to soothe her
and relieve her pain." Tears came to Merah's eyes. "She's
such a good girl!" She kissed her daughter's hands and
thought, "If tears could heal..." as she walked from the
room.

Outside, her husband sat mending a tool. "Is she any
better?" he asked, looking up to Merah.

"No," Merah said sadly, "perhaps worse. Nothing seems
to help." The man reached up and pulled his wife down
beside him. He put his arm around her and she wept
against his broad chest.

"Gods of heaven," Merah prayed out loud,
"gods who heal, gods of the young, why
have you not healed our daughter? We have
brought sacrifices to your altars. We have

chanted your songs. We have promised gifts. Why have you not heard our pleas? Why will you not answer our prayers?"

"Why don't you go to town," Merah's husband told her. "Buy some fruit. Maybe cool fruit will help her fever."

She smiled, hugged him, and went to get her shawl. He rubbed his eyes and again picked up the broken tool, turning it over in his hands to determine how it could be fixed.

As Merah walked down the road toward town, she pondered all that they had done to heal their daughter. They had purchased special herbs and oils. They had talked with neighbors and with the wisest members of their community and tried their remedies. They had prayed for hours at the altars of the gods, and still their daughter's condition worsened. "There is no hope," Merah thought, stopping at a large rock. "She is dying," she sobbed. "My little girl is dying." Merah sat beside the rock, her head on her knees, and wept.

A noise aroused Merah, and she lifted her head to see a group of men and women passing on the road. They were talking with great excitement and she picked up bits from their conversation.

"I couldn't believe it!" one man was saying, "That boy was a cripple all his life and now he walks. It's amazing!"

"That blind man now can see!" another spoke. "Indeed it is amazing!"

A short, wide woman waddled slowly behind the group, mumbling to herself, "Miracles, they were miracles."

"Miracles!" Merah rose from her place by the rock. "A healer? Where?" She ran toward the startled woman.

The short woman looked up at Merah and stepped back. "What would you care, Canaanite?" She said "Canaanite" with the hatred of generations.

"Where can I find this healer?" Merah shouted, grabbing the woman's shawl. "Tell me! Where is this healer?"

Frightened, the woman pulled Merah's hands from her clothing. "He is in town, in a grove of trees beside the fountain. Now leave me alone."

Merah began to run toward the town.

"He won't help you, you know!" the woman shouted after her. "He's a Jew! He will not heal you. He will not even talk to you!" She tossed her head and walked in the opposite direction as fast as her short legs would allow her.

Merah quickly reached the fountain. The sun was beginning to set. It was a time when no woman, Canaanite or Jew, should be out. Nothing, however—no law, no propriety, no religious division—was going to stop Merah.

Now she could see a compound under a cluster of trees a distance from the fountain. Men and women were gathered, and they were beginning to prepare their evening meal around a large campfire. They were indeed Jews. Merah could tell by their clothing and the smell of the food cooking. Merah pulled herself up and lifted her chin to appear strong and composed. She approached the encampment. She had only made a few steps when three men rose from the fire area and strode toward her.

The largest man shouted to her, "What do you want, Canaanite? You are not welcome here."

"I came to see the healer," Merah shouted back with every bit of confidence she had. "I need to see the healer."

"Go to your gods for healing!" another man said. "Our master is resting. Leave us or we will call curses down from our God—the true God—upon you."

Inside herself, Merah shivered, but nothing would stop her. "I am not afraid of your God!" she shouted. "I will not leave! Let me talk to the healer!"

The youngest of the men had left the three and returned to the compound. He now approached Merah and the others. A tall bearded man walked beside him, adjusting his cloak and wiping sleep from his eyes.

"What is the problem here?" he asked. "Can a man not sleep?"

The large man spoke, "I am sorry, Master. This woman refuses to go away."

Merah looked at this "Master." He looked like any other man, but his eyes were kind. Perhaps he would help her. "I am here because you are a healer." Merah pushed against the men who held her back. "My daughter is dying. You have healed others. Heal her, too. I beg you!"

"I am not here to bring life to Canaanites," the healer said. "I am here for the lost sheep of Israel. It is not right to take food from the children and throw it to the dogs."

"She is a child," Merah spoke quietly, almost to herself. "She is just a little girl." Her bold stature left her, her head dropped, and tears again filled her eyes. "Healer," she said humbly, "even the dogs eat the scraps from their master's table."

The healer walked toward her and with his hands wiped the tears from her eyes. He smiled, "Indeed, you are the most persistent woman I have ever met! Your faith is strong, and so is your love for your child. Go! I assure you that your daughter is well and is asking for you."

"I believe you, Master," Merah responded. She turned and ran toward the fountain and the road home, then she stopped and looked back. He was still standing there, watching her.

"Thank you!" she shouted. "You can go rest now."

"Thank you, good woman!" he laughed and put his arm around the man beside him. "Even the dogs..." They laughed and walked back to the fire, the dinner, and their time to rest.

You are merciful, Lord. Help us to know that you always hear our prayer. Help us also to not be afraid to persevere with tenacity as we work for what is needed.

Blessings in Disguise

Theme: Ask and You Shall Receive
Scripture Reflection: Matthew 7:9-11

A continuing prayer throughout my childhood was for a little sister. I was the oldest child in my family, and each time my mother and father shared the news that a baby was on the way, I would begin fervent prayers for a baby girl. In preparation for the answer to my supplication, I would begin to embroider pink bibs, clean up the dolls I planned to pass on, and wash and iron the baby dresses my mother kept in the cedar chest in the basement. I would wait and pray intently until finally, months later, the phone call would come from my father at the hospital. My stature as firstborn gave me the honor of being the first at home to hear the news. "Well, Mary," my dad would say, "you have a new little brother." Sadly, I would put away the pink bib, put the dolls back in my box of old toys, and fold the little dresses I'd prepared and laid out so neatly for when my little sister came home. Out would come the blue sleepers and tiny T-shirts for the baby boy.

I have five brothers. Each is special in his own way. I love them all, but I always felt I was cheated by God for not answering my prayers and giving me a sister.

When I was sixteen, my mother died. The emptiness I felt in her absence was tremendous. A teenage girl needs a mother to learn from, to argue with, to love and to hate, to share stories with, and to rest in when lonely or worried and tired. I felt angry with God that he would snatch my mother away from me when he knew how much I needed her. It wasn't fair.

Several years after our marriage, Jim and I were told that I would not be able to bear children. After several frustrating meetings with social service agencies and learning of the diminishing numbers of infants available for adoption and the costs attached, it seemed that this avenue was closed to us too. Why was God doing this to me? Why was God denying me sisters, a mother, a child?

One evening as I talked long distance to my friend Bonnie I was hit with a revelation. Bonnie and I had met in the fourth grade and become fast friends. Although my family moved to another state when I was thirteen, we still remained best friends. We have grown up together. Through grade school antics, teenage depression, college romances, career plans, marriage, good times and bad times, we have remained close—close like sisters. As I pondered this new realization, I recognized that I have other sisters, people I grew with and grow with still. Thank you, Lord, for the sisters you've given me—for Bonnie and Midge, and Jeannie and Susan, for Helene and Kath!

Then, as if I had new eyes to see, I looked back to the times after my mother died. I looked at Jamie, a neighbor who taught me to cook and shop and organize a home. Jamie was a person with whom I could share my feelings, my hopes, and my dreams, and she is still a close friend. I thought of Beej, a high school teacher who became a guide and mentor, one whom I could argue with and confide in, to rest in when I was weary and lonely. I thought of Eileen, my Confirmation sponsor, a woman who shared the spiritual values and the strong faith my mother had expressed to me in her life. These women weren't the only ones. I realized I had many mothers and friends with whom I am still growing. Thank you, Lord, for the wonderful mothers you have blessed me with: Jamie, Beej, Eileen, Mrs. H., Sue's Mom (no other name would do), Lucia, Aunt Lil.

As I sit here writing this, two little girls sprawl on my living room rug, cutting figures out of a coloring book. No, they're not mine. They are the children of others, but they often come here to play, to talk, to chase the dog, or to watch Tarzan and eat apples in front of the TV. We even had to buy a toybox to keep the playthings of our small friends, our children. I rejoice, Lord, in the gift of children—especially for Stephen, Karen, Sarah, Theresa, Anthony, Christopher, Tiger Jack, John, T.J., Mary Audrey, Martin, and Valerie. Surely God has answered my prayers.

How was it, Lord, that I could not recognize your loving response to my prayers? You have given me more than I asked for. You are generous in your giving, Lord. Help me to recognize all you share with me. Keep my eyes open to your presence and your presents. And please, Lord, bless my sisters, my mothers, my children.

Be Like the Little Children

Theme: Easter
Scripture Reflection: Revelation 19:6

My husband, Jim, and I are ministers of hospitality at our parish. Because of the numerous liturgies and services offered through Holy Week and the Triduum, just about every liturgical minister in our church community was asked to serve at least once. I was asked to work at the Easter Vigil on Saturday night.

The evening was especially hectic. Along with being a greeter/usher for the Vigil, I had been asked to prepare the special reception for the parish, honoring our newly initiated Catholics after Mass. I had spent the afternoon decorating the church basement and preparing food trays. Before I ran upstairs to put on my greeter's nametag, I arranged flowers, filled baskets with crackers and chips, mixed punch, cracked ice, and set up coffee to perk. Now, in the back of the church, there were parishioners to welcome, candles to prepare and distribute, vessels of water to fill, and catechumens to reassure as they anticipated their special role in the evening liturgy.

By nine o'clock the church was full. I found a place in the last pew with the other greeters.

All lights were dimmed and the pastor, outside on the steps, struck a new flame and lit a candle. His light flickered at the back of the church and then passed on to the small candles we held. Soon the dark church began to glow with this new light.

Though the atmosphere was peaceful and the Scriptures were filled with the promises and prophesies fulfilled at Easter's dawn, my mind was moving in another direction. The glory of Christ's resurrection had taken second place to the vegetable dip I had forgotten to prepare and my fears that perhaps I hadn't made enough cheese balls. I was also distracted by a small boy standing beside his mother in the pew ahead. The child was about two, and he had been sitting quietly on his mother's lap, mystified by the candlelight and the peace of the church. Now, however, his attention span spent, he sought to find something else to amuse him. For a while he stood on the pew, looking over the heads to see if anything interesting was happening. He fidgeted and whined. He walked along the seat of the pew, clunking his heavy shoes against the wood.

I was irritated at the child and his mother. A child this young does not belong at a late-night liturgy like this one, I thought. His chattering and clunking distracted the serene and formal ritual. My annoyance finally waned a bit as my mind went back to the reception table and the thought that perhaps I should have purchased yellow napkins instead of white.

Suddenly my thoughts broke as the lights in the church went on. Bells began to ring! Flowers were brought forth to skirt the altar. The choir began to sing the Gloria.

In the pew ahead of me, the little boy's eyes widened. He looked about excitedly to see where all the bells and singing were coming from. Who had turned on all these lights? Look at all the flowers! Why was everybody singing so loudly when it had been so quiet just a few moments ago? He stood on the seat of the pew, turning around in amazement, looking in every direction. Then he threw his tousled head back and laughed. It was that clear, wonderful laugh only a child can express. He clapped his hands and looked at the rest of us to see if we too had recognized the joy of the moment. He looked directly at me as if to say, "Why aren't you laughing, too?"

A light went on inside me. The child was right. Indeed, this was a time to rejoice. My worries vanished as I sang out the Gloria. I understood the exultation expressed in our Easter liturgy: an expression of joy coming from deep within our hearts, a recognition of new light, new hope, an acceptance of new life.

A little boy taught me a special lesson that Easter: a lesson in the joy of our celebration of Jesus' resurrection. A two-year-old gave me new awareness of God's wonderful surprise that in dying we will live. But then, isn't it Jesus who tells us that unless we become like little children, we will not enter the kingdom of heaven?

Thank you, Lord, for wonder, for surprise, and for little children to lead us to you.

The Patron Saint I Never Wanted

Theme: Mary, Mother of Jesus
Scripture Reflection: Luke 1:46-52

It has been the custom in many Catholic families to name the first daughter after Mary, the Mother of God. My mother's mother was Mary Elizabeth. My mother was Helen Marie. My husband's mother is Mary Margaret. Her oldest daughter is Marilyn. I am Mary Adele. It is a long tradition.

No stronger protection, prouder gift, or more powerful blessing was placed upon an infant female than the holy name of Mary. It is a name of strength and holiness—a name that demands respect.

I hated it!

When I began my education in the public schools of San Diego, I met a sea of little girls bearing names like Babs, Bonnie, Suzy, Midge. I longed for a "fun" name. Each summer, when I went to Girl Scout Camp, I made an attempt to take on a new name and get rid of the old Mary. "Mary is my given name," I would tell my counselor, "but everyone calls me Missy." One year the name was Cookie. Another time I told them to call me Cricket. The problem was that I would choose a terrific nickname but forget to answer to it when it was used. The counselors and kids would catch on and pretty soon I was back to Mary.

To me, the name Mary carried a responsibility, a burden that I was somehow forced to tote. You see, unlike the Missys, Cookies, and Crickets who could be wild and foolish and silly whenever they pleased, it seemed to me that Marys were expected to be good examples, hard workers, prayerful daughters, protective sisters, responsible girls. Marys were named after the one who said "Yes" to God; the one who gave birth to the Savior; the one who loved him and taught him; the one who finally knelt at the cross as he died, trusting that he would live again. That's a tough act to follow.

Because of the distance I felt between my namesake and myself, I grew to dislike Mary—both the name and the saint—and sought to separate myself from her image for the sake of my own. In many ways I felt a tension in my relationship with Mary, much like the stress experienced in many mother/daughter relationships. I loved her, yet I hated her. She demanded too much from me. I wasn't her! I did not want to be her!

The images of Mary popular in my childhood contributed to my dislike for her. She was distant, queenly, cool, and sexless. She seemed to be expecting this also from me. One night in 1960, after eighth-grade religion class, a letter was sent home with all the girls. The letter directed the proper dress for us now that we were approaching our teens. A young Catholic woman was expected to wear muted colors, long sleeves, skirts below the knees, and to cover her head when in public. At that time it seemed to me that Mary, Mother of the Church, was requiring her daughters to dress in a way that totally hid their maturing beauty and femininity. They, too, were to be distant, cool, and sexless. I could not do it. Never!

On a warm September afternoon, I and a girlfriend sat reviewing for a quiz on the lawn outside the administration office at my university, when an older priest approached. Offended by our Bermuda shorts, he asked, "Girls, would our Blessed Mother dress in this manner?" Being a Dottie and not a Mary, and therefore unafraid of priestly confrontation, my companion responded, "If she were a young woman today, she probably would." It was the first time I had ever thought of Mary as being a woman—a young woman—like me.

Years had passed since that event, and even though I had made my career in religious education, I made a point of keeping Mary and my mother/daughter conflict with her on a back shelf. I did not want to face again the Mary who would not accept me as I was; the Mary whom I could not accept as model or mother. Because the traditional Marian devotions had lost popularity, I found it fairly easy to avoid the topic of Mary in most of my work. When necessary, I handled Mary in a practical, intellectual manner. I felt strongly that I had outgrown the religious image of Mary; the blue veil, the shimmering crown, the flowery piety always characteristic of her.

Then, a few months ago, I was assigned the task of teaching a class on Mary and her importance in the church for our RCIA program.

"Think about it: Mary on Mary! It'll be great," our pastor asserted. I was stuck with it. I began as a student would approach a term paper: reading, thinking, writing notes. Planning to cover my topic in a remote yet scholarly manner, I was frustrated by the continual interruption of my "relationship" with the woman I studied. Now as I read the Scriptures and the reflections of contemporary thinkers, I began to see Mary in a new way. I saw a Mary without the fairy- blue trappings that always seemed to hide her realness from me. Studying Mary—woman and saint—I began to see a new person altogether. She no longer stood distant, warning me of my humanity. I saw a woman, gentle yet strong, trusting, patient, loving, carrying within her person all the gifts of humanity and offering them openly and fully to God. I was embarrassed to admit to myself that I loved the woman. I admired her. I wanted to be like her. Mary was a woman who gave all that she had—her total humanity, body, and spirit—to serve the Lord. That image calls me as a Christian to give no more and no less than my total self to God. It is an image that does not weigh me down, betraying my humanity, but lifts me up calling me to be me, to be all that I am, to be whole, to be holy, to be Mary.

"Mother, I'm home!"

I thank you, Lord, for models in my life: those who call me to courage, to strength, to hope, and to trust in you.

Reflection and Faith-Sharing

The five spring stories seek to recognize new awareness of God's presence, new gifts, renewed life.

The Clothesline

This story relates our continued linking to our past:
people, tradition, shared faith.

1. What events and persons helped to make you the person that you are? What calls you to be the person you are meant to be?

2. Can you recognize traits, attitudes, responses in you that were also present in your mother, father, grandparents, or other relatives? What are the traditional qualities of your family, both strengths and weaknesses?

A Most Persistent Woman

Persistent tenacity (men call it "nagging")
is a common trait among women, even in our prayer.
In this tale, it proves to be a successful method.

1. Persistence is often seen as a negative quality in women. Have you ever seen persistence as a truly positive act?

2. Can prayer include negative responses to God? Can it include things like anger, failure, depression, frustration, fear, uncertainty? We know that God made us and we know that our personalities include these feelings. Does God still listen to us even when we're not our best?

3. What are you praying most strongly for right now? What are you willing to pray most persistently for?

4. What social issues are you willing to be persistent with? Merah's persistence provided her with a positive answer to her plea of need. Pray and relate with persistence about the issues for which you desire help.

Blessings in Disguise

Sometimes the answers to your prayer are standing out right in front of you, but for some reason you just can't recognize them.

1. Consider in prayer those things you have always wanted, wished for, hoped for, prayed for.

2. Reflect on what you have received in answer to those hopes and prayers. Try not to be negative. Look for the positive.

3. Do you have a story to share that relates a special answer to a prayer, but wasn't the answer you had been expecting or desiring?

Be Like the Little Children

Sometimes age and practicalities blind us to all that is before us.

1. What has a child taught you lately? How is a child's response to events different from yours?

2. You still have some childlike qualities, don't you? Reflect on these for a moment. Consider how these qualities might bring you closer to God and to God's presence in your life.

The Patron Saint I Never Wanted

This story relates the importance of finding humanity as well as divinity in our Lord and in the saints.

1. What makes it difficult for us to see Jesus and the saints as real people—people who felt human feelings and concerns? Is it important to see them as people like us? What are your thoughts about the saints?

2. Do you have a favorite saint? In what ways is this person an example of faith to you?

3. Do you have any negative feelings toward a particular saint? Where does those feelings come from?

4. Do a little research on a favorite saint.

SUMMER

Let the heavens be glad and the earth rejoice;
let the sea and what fills it resound;
let the plains be joyful and all that is in them!
Then shall all the trees of the forest exult
before the LORD,...for he comes to rule the earth.
Psalm 96:11-13

Squawker and Grey

Theme: Parents, Teachers, Guides
Scripture Reflection: Isaiah 40:31

I was on my hands and knees, pulling up weeds in the backyard, when I first heard the squawking. I really didn't think much about it at first, but when several minutes went by and the racket didn't stop, I began to look for its source.

In the corner of the yard, on a thick branch in the apple tree, sat a speckled bird. Its feathers were ruffled, its mouth was wide open, and it was squawking. The din was so sharp and piercing that I wondered if the poor creature was hurt. I was considering going closer when I noticed a second, larger bird in the tree. This bird was a soft grey. It sat calmly about two feet from the source of the noise, watching it closely. In its mouth, the grey bird held a crushed beetle, and though the beetle did not look at all tasty to me, it was obviously what the squawker wanted.

"This is an interesting situation," I thought, as I settled in to observe. "Perhaps they'll fight it out."

The grey bird continued to sit calmly on her limb, not at all agitated by the din created by the squawker. Occasionally, Grey would jump closer and tilt her head, revealing more of the beetle to Squawker, then hop back to her original branch. Squawker wouldn't move. He only squawked more.

I had been watching for several minutes when Squawker began to flap his speckled wings and fluttered awkwardly to a limb closer to Grey. Immediately Grey hopped forward and gave the beetle to Squawker!

"A-ha! I understand! This large speckled baby is being taught to fly," I thought.

That entire afternoon, as I attacked my dandelions and crabgrass, I observed the interaction between Squawker and Grey. I became frustrated by Squawker's inability to understand that it wasn't the making of noise that brought him food, but the movement of his wings. I was impressed by Grey's gentle patience and persistence. She never seemed weakened by the din. She knew her task, and with great tenacity she stayed with it.

By the time I was gathering up the clumps of dead weeds scattered over the lawn, Squawker had moved—coaxed by Grey and her tasty bug delights—from the boughs of the apple tree to the top of the redwood fence. And as I raked around my shrubs, I watched as Squawker made a giant leap from the fence to my neighbor's oak tree about twenty feet away. "Hooray, Squawker!" I shouted and clapped my hands.

"Hooray, what?" my husband asked as he walked into the yard.

"It's hard to explain," I responded. He shrugged his shoulders and we went into the house.

As I sat in church that evening, waiting for mass to begin, my mind went back to Squawker and Grey, and I began to reflect on the Squawkers and Greys that have touched my life. My mother was a wonderful Grey—patient and persistent. She helped me to develop many skills and abilities I would need to survive happily in this crazy world. In my own Squawker stage, I was blessed by many teachers and friends who urged me on in the development of my gifts and extension of my possibilities.

I recalled the many Squawkers in my life, too. In the years that I taught high school, I remember the various tasty bugs I held before flightless students. I remember the joy of seeing the beginnings of flight and rejoicing in their first experience of lofty soaring.

Growth, it seems, is never easy. Each time we are called to accept a greater endeavor, don't we do a certain amount of squawking? Changing, growing, stretching is always hard and often painful. So many times we owe our growth to those who sat gently and patiently as we squawked, urging us on. They knew what we could achieve.

As the processional hymn began, I thanked God for all the Greys who had touched my life and who continue to help me to be all that I am called to be. I also asked his blessing on the Squawkers I have touched and those that will come before me in the future.

Thank you, Lord, for the guides you have given me through these years. Bless them. Help me, Lord to be a patient teacher and mentor for the Squawkers with whom I have been blessed.

Becky's Butterfly

Becky Blanton, parish housekeeper, cantor, mother of three, and good friend, proudly entered the church offices early last fall, carrying a canning jar full of dark green leaves. Pulling a large piece of gauze from our first-aid kit and flapping it in the air, she announced to all within hearing range that on one of these leaves she'd found a tiny black egg. Within a few days, she assured us, a tiny caterpillar will appear. The caterpillar will eat all the leaves, grow to be about two inches long, shed its striped skin to form into a pale green chrysalis, and about eight days later break forth as a monarch butterfly! She covered the jar with the gauze and a rubber band, set it on the work counter between a stack of catalogs and the paper cutter, and left.

"She's crazy!" Charlotte, our parish secretary, commented. We all nodded and went back to work. How could someone know all this from a tiny black dot on a dark green leaf?

101

However, within two days we noticed a minute
caterpillar munching on a leaf when we came in to work.
We moved the jar to a more prominent spot and spent
our coffee breaks observing its inhabitant's progress. By
the end of the week, the caterpillar had a name, Ralph,
and had grown to be about two striped inches. He'd eaten
all the leaves, and Becky was bringing him fresh ones
sprinkled with water. We watched Ralph drink water
drops off the leaves each morning.

One rainy Thursday after lunch, we noticed that Ralph
had attached himself to the gauze netting and was hanging
upside-down in his jar above the leaves. All afternoon we
watched him writhe as he slowly shed his striped skin
until it fell like a dark crumpled rag to the bottom of the
jar and was covered with leaves.

Ralph was gone now, and from the gauze hung a pale
green chrysalis dotted with a row of metallic gold specks.
There was no movement at all. The chrysalis hung still like
a small jade carving.

"It will be about eight days until he comes out as a
butterfly," Becky told us. We were believing her now, and
Charlotte designed a sheet for us to predict the day and
time of Ralph's rebirth. We began taking bets.

When we came into work on Friday of the next week,
the chrysalis had turned deep brown. We were ready for
this; Becky had instructed us that this would be the sign
that Ralph's breakout was imminent.

That afternoon, as Charlotte and I began folding flyers
and stuffing envelopes, we moved Ralph's jar to our work
table so that we could watch for his emergence. Around

two o'clock, the dark chrysalis began to move. Its upper half split, and a new creature started to appear. The process was exhausting. The butterfly worked to gain a greater degree of freedom, then had to rest a bit before struggling once more. "I think I'd stay a caterpillar," Charlotte said with a sigh.

Finally, at 4:30, a damp, wrinkled butterfly hung from the gauze. Within a few moments, wings were stretched and flapped dry.

At five o'clock, the entire office staff watched Christopher, Becky's youngest, walk out to the office courtyard with the resurrected Ralph perched on his finger. After taking a moment to test the wind, and amid great applause, Ralph took to the air in search of the sweet nectar of fall flowers.

We shared wine together, toasting Ralph's new growth and the end of summer. Each commented on the apparent pain involved in Ralph's change from caterpillar to butterfly. "I hope it was worth it!" Charlotte said. "I'm sure it is," Becky replied. "Just look."

The courtyard, deep green with the long shadows of early evening, sparkled now with a number of orange and black butterflies enjoying the warmth, enjoying the flowers, enjoying the freedom each had patiently struggled for.

Sometimes, Lord, it seem like things will never change and that growth will never occur. Help me to know that your plan is a plan of constant growth—growth toward new life and resurrection.

"My Name is Abigail"

Theme: Covenant of Marriage
Scripture Reflection: Song of Songs 8:6-7

My name is Abigail. I think you know my husband, Simon the fisherman. Yes, that's him. Some call him Peter. I knew that you knew him! His name is recognized in so many places now! So much has happened over these past years. It's hard to say exactly when it all began. Let me think.

You know, I can't remember a time when I did not know Simon. We lived in the same little town. His mother and my mother had been good friends since they were girls. His father was a fisherman. I was thirteen when our families arranged our marriage. He was sixteen—a large man even then—with big hands and dark, curly hair. I recall the evening when he came formally to our house to share the Sabbath meal with us. Poor Simon, except for responding to Papa's prayers, he didn't say a word. I don't think he ever even looked up from his plate that evening. I know he didn't look at me, and I barely looked at him. I do remember that he enjoyed Mama's food! I also noticed that though he was young, his hands were already rough from working with the nets. And I do recall, as I sat beside him, that he smelled like fish.

After our meal, Papa suggested that we go for a walk together to get acquainted. I remember how quiet we were as we walked that first time. We went through the streets of the village toward the sea, both looking down, carefully watching our feet, sure that everyone was observing us. Simon seemed to relax as we got closer to the water. The moon was full and bright in the evening sky. There were many noisy gulls still flying about, fighting over the unacceptable fishes tossed from the nets. Silver-edged waves lapped onto the rocky beach.

When we came to the shore, Simon stopped and leaned against a large rock. He stretched, smiled, took off his sandals, and dug his toes into the sand. I slipped my shoes off, too, and we walked on the wet sand, close together along the edge of the water.

"I am a fisherman," he said.

(As if I didn't know! His father was a fisherman, as his grandfather and great-grandfather had been. His little brother, Andrew, was already learning to fold sails and to mend and dry the nets.)

"I will be master of my father's boat and nets someday."

I smiled.

"Fishermen need to be up very, very early." He seemed to raise himself a few inches taller as he spoke. "We cast our nets long before dawn and fish with only the light of the moon and the stars to guide us."

(My mother always called me The Sleepy One. Imagine me up before dawn preparing food for a hungry husband!)

I sighed.

"I am a good man, Abigail," he stopped, looking out at the sea and then to me. "I will care for you and our children. I will be faithful to God and to our marriage covenant."

It was the first time I had noticed how deep and dark his eyes were—dark like the sea at night with a sparkle of distant stars.

"I am a sleepy one, Simon. But I will work to serve you and care for you and our children. I will be faithful to God and to our marriage covenant."

He took my hand. "Come!" he beamed. "Let me show you my father's boat. I will show you the nets." He took my hand and we ran down the beach.

We were married in a wonderful celebration and had our first and only child almost a year later. We named our child Jonah, after Simon's father. Little Jonah was Simon's treasure! They would laugh and play together, and when he was only five, Jonah would go with Simon out to the sea early in the morning to fish with him and to watch the stars. On especially bright mornings, I could see them out on the water, Jonah sitting at the bow of his father's boat, helping with the sails.

Jonah grew very ill when he was barely nine. People from our town who were skilled in medicine came to help us. We made offerings to God, praying for healing. We did everything we could to make the boy well. Nothing helped. Simon sat for hours beside the boy's bed. One night, holding the child's small hands in his own, Simon said, "When you are well, my little Jonah, we will go together once again out on the blue waters to fish and see the stars sparkle in the dark sky." At dawn that morning, Jonah died in Simon's arms. I remember that for almost a month Simon did not fish. He spent much time walking on the shore and talking with God.

As time went on the pain seemed to ease. Simon and his brother went back to work. Though he was still kind and gentle with me, my husband was no longer close. He was distant and tired, angry and brooding. The sparkle was gone from my love's eyes.

Everything changed one brilliant summer morning when Simon and Andrew burst into our home. The sun had been up for hours. I was becoming concerned about what was delaying Simon's return from the sea when I heard them running up the road to the house.

"Abby!" Simon shouted, "Abby come look." Quickly I covered my head and left the house. "Look, Abby, look! Look down at the catch!"

There, spread on racks on the shore below was the greatest catch of fish I had ever seen.

"Children!" Andrew called, "Come quickly! Look what your Papa and Uncle Simon caught today. Go down and help to clean the fish. Daniel and Benjamin ran down the hill. Hannah, only four, toddled after them. "Watch your sister," I called out.

"I have food for you, Simon. Come join us, Andrew. Tell me about this lucky catch."

Simon caught me around the waist. "I cannot eat. I cannot think. We met a man—a man from Nazareth—a teacher, an amazing teacher.

"Amazing is not the word." Andrew, breathless, excited, and exhausted, sat down. "A man, a stranger, called us as we were coming in. All night we had caught next to nothing. We were tired. This man was sitting on the rocks, shaking sand out of his shoes. He called to us to throw out our nets. We just laughed at him. What a fool! But he called again to throw out the nets and get a great catch.

"Simon said to me, 'Let's show this fool that he knows nothing' and flung his net onto the water as if it were a dancer's scarf. Suddenly the sea bubbled with fish! I threw my net out broadly and more fish appeared. We pulled in more than our boat could hold. Those at the shore saw us and brought their boats out. We filled all the boats with our great catch." Andrew leaned back and sighed, "Then the teacher said to us,..." he paused, taking a deep breath. "He said, 'Leave your nets...'"

Simon took my hands and his voice diminished to a whisper. "The man said, 'Leave your nets and come with me. I will make you fishers of men.'"

I pulled my hands from Simon's and placed bread and bowls of fruit before the men. "Leave your nets?"

Simon looked up, took my hands again, and said, "Yes, Abby. In two days Andrew and I must go."

My heart began to pound sharply and I felt dizzy. I could not understand what was happening, except that for the

first time in four years I saw stars sparkling in my
husband's eyes.

All day I watched Simon as he pulled his boat up from
the shore and folded his sails and his nets, laying them in
the shade beside the house. I mended his cloak and chose
the best of our dried fish for him to carry. That night, as I
lay beside him, I listened to the familiar rhythm of his
breathing. I ached thinking of him leaving. I prayed for
strength and wisdom. I prayed that God would care for
him. I prayed that this would not be the last night I felt his
warm body against mine.

Long before dawn, I was awakened by my mother's
grating cough. Mama had always been a frail woman and
now, in her old age, she had grown ill and barely able to
care for herself. I left my bed, poured water from a pitcher
into a cup and brought it to her. She took a few sips and
looked at my face. "My Abigail!" She shook her head. "Are
you in pain?"

"No, Mama," I assured her. "I am only sad that my
Simon will be leaving tomorrow to follow the Teacher. I
am missing him already." Tears came into my eyes.

"I would like to meet this Teacher." Mama coughed,
"Invite him here to eat tonight. I will help cook." She
coughed again and took another drink of water from the
cup in my hand.

"You are too sick to cook, but..." I thought a moment.
"It would be nice to meet the Teacher. I will ask Simon to
bring him home to share our supper. I will make a special
meal—Simon's favorite—for his final night in our home."

I felt full of life and energy that day. I prepared a feast fit for a wedding. That evening, as the sun was setting, my home was full. Andrew was there with his wife, Rebecca, and their children. Other men, also followers of the Teacher, sat about sharing stories. I served a fine meal with warm bread, meat and sauce, fruit, and wine.

As the evening continued, the men sat and talked of their plans and hopes. Rebecca had taken the children home to bed. I had given Mama her dinner and she was sleeping. Now alone, cleaning up after the meal, I couldn't hold my tears back. Leaning away from the doorway, my whole body ached with loneliness. Already I missed my Simon. I was angry with the Teacher. I was angry with God.

My face against the wall, I felt a presence behind me. A hand touched my shoulder. Sure that it was Simon, I reached up and grasped it tightly. I turned to find the Teacher before me.

"Abigail, wife of Simon, you made a fine meal," he said. "Thank you for preparing it for us."

I dropped my head, not wanting him to see my tears. He bent his knees slightly, lowering himself to look at my face. "Why are you sad, Daughter? What brings those tears to your eyes?"

"My husband will be leaving tomorrow," I told him. "My heart is breaking with the thought of his absence."

"Come with me, Abigail, wife of Simon. We need you with us. We need you to pray with us and share our work. Truly, wife of Simon, we need someone to care for us." He smiled and my heart leapt with excitement until I heard my mother's cough. I sighed and lowered my eyes again.

"My mother is ill," I told him softly. "I cannot leave her."

"Your mother is not ill," he said. "Look! She comes now to help you with your work."

I turned to see Mama enter the room. She looked like a different woman. Warm color had returned to her face. She stood tall, no longer bent over. She smiled and embraced me, then stood before the Teacher. "God bless you, Teacher, and bless the mother that bore you." She kissed his hands.

"See," he said to me. "Your mother is well. Come with us, Abigail."

Mama grinned and began stacking the dishes. "Go, Abigail," she said. "Nothing stops you."

The days and weeks that followed were amazing. Though I was the first woman to travel with this rugged group, I was not the only one. As we traveled and the Teacher spoke, others joined our group. I met people different from those in my hometown of Bethsaida. There were a few children and a number of women, companions to their husbands, brothers, or sons. There was a woman the Teacher had saved from stoning, a youth to whom he had given sight, and a man who had once been a leper. There were two women who, after hearing the Teacher, knew that their lives could never be the same and left their homes and the protection of their families to be close to this man and his followers. We had little, but we were happy together. Each day we shared work and prayer. We laughed much and shared many dreams and hopes. In the evening, around the fire, the Teacher would tell us stories of the Kingdom of God, our Father and protector. My love and respect for my husband grew as I observed his deep devotion to the Teacher.

It was in our final trip to Jerusalem that things began to change drastically. It is hard to express the feelings we had as we approached the holy city. Deep joy and expectation was in our hearts. We knew that the kingdom was very near. Yet among us there was also deep, deep fear. Rumors ran wild: the best, that the Teacher would be recognized by all of Israel as King; the worst, that all of us would be arrested and killed.

Our entrance into the city the day before the Passover was exciting. The day was brilliant. Almond trees blossomed and flowers dressed the once-dead fields in myriad color. All our friends from Jerusalem had gathered with others from the city. The Teacher entered joyfully, riding on a donkey. It was like a parade as people sang and waved green palms, laying them down on the dusty road.

We set up our camp outside a grove of olive trees. Simon and one of the other men had been sent ahead to prepare a room for our Passover feast. We set our fires to heat the flat stones we carried to make our bread. James, one of the group, slaughtered our finest lamb and brought it to us for cooking. Matthew and Andrew went into the city to buy wine and spices. Children gathered fruit and herbs.

While I sat chopping apples for sauce, I recalled sitting as a child next to my grandmother as she prepared these foods, reminding us of our passing from slavery to freedom. It was a joyful time for all of us as we linked our past to our present, reaching into a new future.

The meal was wonderful. The mother of Thaddeus, being the oldest of our group, blessed and lit the Passover candles. Mary of Magdala poured wine from large stone pitchers. John Mark, almost ready for his Bar Mitzvah, asked the question, "How is this night different from any other night?" We ate and drank and sang and danced together.

At the end of the feast, the Teacher took the last piece of unleavened bread—the Afikomen, the bread of redemption—and broke it. He looked at us, his eyes piercing the candlelit room. "This is my body," he said, "This is for you, for your redemption. And this," he lifted the final cup of wine, "is my blood poured out like that of the paschal lamb to give you true freedom from slavery."

I must confess that at the time we did not understand at all what he was saying.

The men left and, after cleaning up, the women returned to our compound of tents. We were all exhausted, weak from work, wine, and celebration. I do not know how long I had been asleep before I was awakened by shouting and screams.

Temple guards had approached the men's sleeping area. I was told that the Teacher had been arrested. I searched for Simon. All the men were gone. Mary of Magdala told me that Simon had followed behind the guards to see what would happen. She led us into the grove of olives. We carried the sleeping children with us and together we prayed through the night, the sleeping children cuddled at our feet.

Shortly after the sun rose, I saw my Simon leaning against a tree on the other side of the grove. As I approached and called to him, he looked away, ashamed. I touched his shoulder and he turned and fell like a child into my arms.

"Leave me, Abby," he wept. "I am a terrible man! I have abandoned my Teacher, my Master! He is in grave danger, and in my fear, I denied him and ran away." He could say no more. He wept until he fell into a restless sleep. I held him, praying for God's power to protect the Teacher and his love and strength to calm my husband.

I am sure you know the rest of our story. I cannot explain the tragic though wondrous events that occurred. Each of us was changed by the pouring out of our Teacher's blood. The power we gained in understanding his teaching and recalling his stories amazes me still. More people have been healed. More members have joined our community, and we have traveled in many lands.

Simon, now called Peter the Rock by our community, has become the leader, the Papa of our group. He works very hard and must travel a great deal. We are together sometimes, and though I miss him when we are apart, I can still feel his love and his presence.

The last time we were together, we were in Ortona, a city on the sea in the Roman world. I remember us walking together down the rocky streets and onto the shore. There, Simon stopped, ran his hand through his shaggy gray hair, and resting on a large stone, removed his worn sandals and dug his toes into the sand. "I'm a fisherman," he smiled, taking my hand. "Come, Ill show you my father's boat!" I laughed, took his hand, and looked up into his eyes. They were so dark, like the midnight sky over the Sea of Galilee, sparkling with stars.

Lord, give me courage to face the many changes that will come into my life. Help me to remain faithful to my covenant with you and with my love.

Taste and See

Theme: Encouraging Good Growth
Scripture Reflection: Ezekiel 17:8

When I was a little girl and my father was a student on the GI Bill at the University of Utah, summers were special to me. Because jobs were difficult to find in Salt Lake and because my mother missed her family in South Dakota, we would travel each summer to the tiny town of Agar and for three months raise its population from 104 to 107 (108 after my brother John was born).

During those months we would live on my grandparents' farm. My father would work the farm with Grandpa. My mother would help feed family and farmhands as well as keep track of me and my young cousins while we explored old sheds and barns, tasted wild berries and fruits, played with dogs and cats, sheep, cows, and chickens, and generally enjoyed being children of creation.

It was wonderful. In my opinion, the most wonderful part of those days was my grandfather. He was my hero, my best friend, an amazing man who could find the pale green spotted eggs in a field sparrow's nest hidden under a clump of tall grass, call out to sheep and pigs and have them come, and drive big tractors and trucks. While milking cows, Grandpa could even aim squirts of milk right into the open mouths of six or seven farmcats who would sit in a row against the barn wall each morning and evening. Whenever possible I was at Grandpa's side, wearing blue denim overalls just like his and following his big footsteps with my little ones.

One evening, after Grandma's fine supper of fried chicken and apple pie, Grandpa got up from the table and announced that he was taking his walk. I slid off my chair, took his hand, and we walked out of the house.

It was a beautiful evening, quiet and warm with long dark shadows stretching out from under the row of cottonwood trees that separated the house and farm buildings from the road and fields. We went past the windmill and its big, mossy green water tank, plucked a few currents from Grandma's berry bushes that ran along the wire fence, tossed a few small rocks at birds in the yard by the chickenhouse, and crossed the road to walk into a newly plowed field.

The soft clods of earth were large, making it hard to keep up with Grandpa. When we finally reached the center of the field, Grandpa stopped and looked around. I did, too. Grandpa stooped down, looking at the moist dirt. I stooped down too. Grandpa picked up a handful of soil and sifted it through his fingers. So did I. Then he took a pinch of earth and put it in his mouth.

At four years old, I knew you weren't supposed to put dirt in your mouth!

"Mama says not to eat dirt, Grandpa!" I told him emphatically.

He spit the dirt out. "I'm not eating it." He spit again. "I'm tasting it. I'm seeing what it needs before I plant my winter wheat."

Many years later, as I sat at a battered folding table in a church hall with St. Mary's parish council, the experience of that evening with Grandpa came back to me. It had been an especially difficult meeting. Each member seemed to have a different plan, a different idea about what the parish needed. We had so little money. Nothing seemed clear to us. What did we really need? What could we honestly offer? What did we need to supply in order to get things going?

"I think we need to taste the dirt," I said under my breath.

"Huh?" Bill Patterson, our council president, asked.

"Oh, it's nothing," I responded. "I was just thinking about how my Grandfather determined what was good and present and what was needed in the soil before he planted his crops."

The group was ready for any kind of break. "What did he do?" one of the members inquired. "My uncle's a farmer. He took lots of biology and chemistry classes in college to help him determine soil needs. Farmers today can get pretty specific."

"My grandfather just tasted the dirt," I said, sharing the story. "He just tasted the dirt, and things always seemed to grow."

"Maybe that's what we need to do," Bill mused, leaning back. "Maybe there's a way we can taste our soil here and learn what we have that's good and strong in this parish and what needs to be added to help in this year's growth. Let's pray about it, and talk at our next meeting."

As we left the parking lot, I noticed the quiet warm evening and the long shadows of the trees that graced the west side of the church. "Help us to taste the good strengths and needs of this parish, Grandpa. Help us to get good growth here." I smiled, and for just a moment I felt a large hand touching my small one with love.

Lord, may we be fertile soil in which your love and mercy may grow strong. Allow us to bear fruit that can nourish the hungry, comfort the oppressed, bring home the lonely and the alienated, and make present your Kingdom with justice, love, and peace forever.

A Litany for You and Me

Theme: A Prayer for Assistance
Scripture Reflection: Psalm 89:5

I began this book with a dedication litany, a prayer
requesting God's good blessings upon the people who
have filled and continue to fill my life with purpose and
love. I thought it would be appropriate to end this book
and this warm season of summer with the Lord by sharing
another litany, a litany calling for the support of many of
our special patron saints. This is a prayer for all of us who
continue to strive to know and serve the Lord: workers,
parents, teachers, children, ministers. We are people of
many ages, cultures, and traditions. We hold many hopes
and seek many goals. Together we are Family. We are
Church. We are People of God and Body of Christ. In
this closing prayer, we ask for the guidance and assistance
of the saints who gave witness to
their faith and even now lead and
inspire us.

Work is good, and all are called to labor in your vineyards, Lord. For direction in our work we pray:

St. James, Patron of Laborers . . . . Inspire us

St Ferdinand III, Patron of Engineers . . . . Inspire us

St. Thomas More, Patron of Lawyers . . . . Inspire us

St. Isadore, Patron of Farmers . . . . Inspire us

Sts. Cosmos and Damien, Patrons of Doctors . . . . Inspire us

St. Vincent Ferrer, Patron of Builders . . . . Inspire us

St. Florian, Patron of Firefighters . . . . Inspire us

St. Michael, Patron of Grocers and Police Officers . . Inspire us

St. Genesius, Patron of Secretaries . . . . Inspire us

St. Agatha, Patron of Nurses . . . . Inspire us

St. John Gualbert, Patron of Forest Workers . . . . Inspire us

St. Hadrian, Patron of Soldiers . . . . Inspire us

St. Gregory, Patron of Teachers . . . . Inspire us

St. Louise de Marillac, Patron of Social Workers . . . Inspire us

St. Albert, Patron of Scientists . . . . Inspire us

St. John Vianney, Patron of Parish Priests . . . . . Inspire us

St. Martha, Patron of Servants . . . . Inspire us

St. Anne, Patron of Homemakers . . . . Inspire us

We know that our lives cannot always be easy, free of worry, and filled with joy. As we are faced with difficulties we pray:

St. Anthony of Padua, Patron of the Poor . . . . . Assist us

St. Barbara, Patron of Prisoners . . . . Assist us

St. John of God, Patron of the Sick . . . . Assist us

St. Alphonsus Liguori, Patron of Confessors . . . . Assist us

St. Dympha, Patron of the Mentally Ill . . . . . . Assist us

St. Ansovinus, Protector of Crops . . . . Assist us

St. Matthew, Patron of Tax Collectors . . . . Assist us

St. Catherine of Alexandria, Patron of Jurists . . . . Assist us

Holy Innocents, Patron of the Abandoned . . . . . Assist us

St. Odilia, Patron of the Blind . . . . Assist us

St. Roch, Patron of Invalids . . . . Assist us

St. Anthony, Patron of Lost Articles . . . . Assist us

St. Peregrine, Patron of those with Cancer . . . . . Assist us

St. Frances de Sales, Patron of the Deaf . . . . . . Assist us

St. Vincent de Paul, Patron of Charity . . . . Assist us

St. Theresa of Avila, Patron of Headache Sufferers . . Assist us

St. Peter of Alcantara, Patron of Watchmen . . . . . Assist us

St. Camillus de Lellis, Patron of Hospitals . . . . . Assist us

St. Jude, Patron of Desperate Circumstances . . . . Assist us

St. Joan of Arc, Patron of Courage . . . . Assist us

Lord, you have called us to show love and concern for our community: our families, our friends, our co-workers, all the people who touch our lives and our thoughts daily. So, for good guidance, we call on our Saints, our sources of true inspiration, asking:

Mary, Mother of God . . . . Pray for us

St. Valentine, Patron of Greetings . . . . Pray for us

St. Monica, Patron of Mothers . . . . Pray for us

St. Joseph, Patron of Fathers . . . . Pray for us

St. Nicholas, Patron of Children . . . . Pray for us

St. Gerard Majella, Patron of Expectant Mothers . . . Pray for us

St. Lawrence, Patron of Cooks . . . . Pray for us

St. George, Patron of Boys . . . . Pray for us

St. Agnes, Patron of Girls . . . . Pray for us

St. John Bosco and St. Maria Goretti,
   Patrons of Teenagers . . . . Pray for us

St. Thomas Aquinas, Patron of Students . . . . . . Pray for us
St. Charles Borromeo, Patron of Seminarians . . . . Pray for us
St. Raphael, Patron of Lovers . . . . Pray for us

And in our times of relaxation, as we seek rest and renewal, we pray:

St. Dorothy, Patron of Gardeners . . . . Renew us
St. Honoratus, Patron of Bakers . . . . Renew us
St. Luke, Patron of Artists . . . . Renew us
St. David, Patron of Poets . . . . Renew us
St. Cecelia, Patron of Musicians . . . . Renew us
St. Gregory, Patron of Singers . . . . Renew us
St. Genesius, Patron of Actors . . . . Renew us
St. Ambrose, Patron of Learning . . . . Renew us
St. Bernard, Patron of Skiers . . . . Renew us
St. Francis of Assisi, Patron of Ecologists . . . . . . Renew us
St. Brendan, Patron of Sailors . . . . Renew us
St. George, Patron of Scouting . . . . Renew us
St. Francis of Rome, Patron of Automobiles . . . . . Renew us
St. Christopher, Patron of Travelers . . . . Renew us
St. Clare of Assisi, Patron of Television . . . . . . Renew us
St. Sebastian, Patron of Athletes . . . . Renew us
St. Ignatius Loyola, Patron of Retreats . . . . . . Renew us
St. Anthony Abbott, Patron of Pets . . . . Renew us
St. Andrew, Patron of Fishermen . . . . Renew us
St. Eutachius, Patron of Hunters . . . . Renew us
St. Amand, Patron of Innkeepers . . . . Renew us
St. Vita, Patron of Humor . . . . Renew us

Finally, I pray for the encouragement of the saints who have blessed my life—the people who have personally touched me with their goodness, their witness, their love, and their direction. Though they are gone from me now, their remembrance and spiritual presence still guides me. Remember them as I do now:

For my grandfather, Edward McEntee, who shared wonderful stories and deeply loved his family, especially his grandchildren. Continue to inspire me with stories of love and goodness, Grandpa.

For my grandmother, Matey Bennett McEntee, who taught me the love of all living things: birds and animals, flowers, plants, trees, and most importantly, people. Continue to thrill me with the wonder of all creation, Grandma.

For my grandfather, Erhardt Doerr, who shared with me the incredible beauty of all growing things. Continue to reveal to me the special virtue of nature.

For my mother, Helen Doerr McEntee, who taught me to be patient and to love deeply, who continues to call me to be a good woman and a loving wife. Continue to guide me, Mama.

For my grandmother, Mary Salvatori Doerr, who was always there to offer milk, bread, and a warm kitchen. Help me, Grandma, to always open my home to others.

For my aunt, Geraldine McEntee Sable, who shared a beautiful sense of humor and wonderful artistic ability. Aunt Gerry, inspire me to express God's love through laughter and to cherish the joy of drawing.

For my teacher, mentor, and friend, B.J. Montag, who encouraged me to always do my best and to face life with independence, courage, and perseverance. Continue to help me to face life with gentle strength, Beej.

For my cousin, Patrick McEntee, a teenage boy who will continue to be a sign for me of youthful energy and excitement. Energize me, Pat!

For Ricky Gonzalez, whose strength, boldness and animation cannot be stifled even by death. Be my protector, Ricky.

For my friend, Geri Morgan, who planted pansies, shared tea, and faced death with equal gentleness and grace. Bring me courage, Geri.

For little Jack LaValley, whose infant death reminds me always that life is a gift to be treasured, day by day, minute by minute. Jack, keep me aware of the goodness of life.

And for all others—friends and foes—who now stand in the full presence of the Lord, continue to bless the lives of those of us who stand in trepidation as we anticipate our final unity with our one Father in Heaven.

Amen! Amen!

Reflection and Faith-Sharing

The warm, play-filled season of summer celebrates growth and the unfolding of life's beauty and fruitfulness. Summer's stories can remind us to take time to reflect upon our continuing growth as we travel along our road of faith and to stop every once in a while and enjoy what we have accomplished.

Squawker and Grey

Teaching is not easy, nor is learning.
These take time, patience, and persistence. Those who teach also deserve a little rejoicing over their achievement.

1. Recall a "Grey" in your life—someone who took time to teach you, to assist you in accomplishing a task or refining a skill. Spend some time remembering this person, the qualities he or she held, and the way this person responded to your growth and development.

2. Spend time considering God's role in your continued growth and development. Reflect on God's encouragement, your "Grey" urging you on.

3. Now recall a special "Squawker"—someone you were called to teach or to assist in his or her growth and understanding. Remember this person in prayer for a moment.

4. How is God calling you now to help in the growth of another individual? What assistance will you need to accomplish your task?

5. How is God calling you to greater growth? Who is present to you?

Becky's Butterfly

Resurrection is painful as well as beautiful.

1. No one believed Becky when she entered with the jar of leaves. Have you been surprised when something good occurred that you felt would never happen? Consider what allowed this event to come about.

2. Recall a time of great pain in your life. How were you changed by this experience for good and for bad? How did you grow?

3. Because of your experience with pain, are there ways that you are able to help others who must go through this type of suffering? Consider the possibility of God calling you in the special ministry.

4. Remember the occasion of passing through pain to growth. How was this occasion celebrated? In prayer, respond joyfully to your growth.

5. Pray about the joy you obtained through your growth.

My Name is Abigail

Abigail's story is one of fidelity. Her covenant and her love give her the commitment to stand in strength and in confidence alongside her husband in spite of the radical change of his life.

1. When have you been called to stand strongly beside an individual—a spouse, a friend, a public, or a religious leader? What were your feelings? Your fears and unease? What encouraged you to continue to stand with this person?

2. Have you ever felt called to uphold with strength and faithfulness an issue, cause, political or religious stand? What were your feelings? What gave you strength to make this stand?

3. Are you being called by God now to make a stand confidently and faithfully for a person or for a cause? Pray about what you need to do this.

4. In accomplishing a task that took strong faith and commitment, did you take time along the way to forgive, to love, to rest, to celebrate? Do you need to do this now?

Taste and See

This is a good story to use when you stand at the edge of planning—when you are taking a deep breath before you jump in.

1. Many people become frustrated with initial planning. They feel it is a waste of their good time. Some people seem to spend all their time planning and never get to the doing. Reflect on your experiences with planning and achievement.

2. Have you ever been in a situation where you jumped into something without any preparation and found that things were nothing like you thought they would be? Consider what you learned from this.

3. Can you recall a situation when you had to "taste and see" before you could begin your work? Reflect upon that situation and what was learned.

4. How is God a part of your planning and doing?

A Litany for You and Me

This final prayer will remind you that you are definitely not alone on your journey of faith. The Church's patrons can inspire and encourage you in all areas of your work and growth.

1. Choose the patron saints who relate most closely to your life and design make a small litany just for you. (Don't forget to include St. Vita, Patron of Humor!)

2. In your prayers, remember to recall your own saints—your parents or grandparents, friends and loved ones who are now with God. Their love and concern for you did not end with their death. Their example is still alive in your memory.

Scripture Index

Theme Index

OTHER GOOD STORIES
FOR INVITING FAITH-SHARING

THE LIGHT IN THE LANTERN
True Stories for Your Faith Journey
by James L. Henderschedt
Paperbound $8.95, 124 pages, 5 ½" x 8 ½"
ISBN 0-89390-209-8

This collection, linked to the lectionary, goes beyond facts to the "truth" of your faith journey. Use them for personal reflection, homily preparation, or small-group work. "Dennis Meets St. Peter" will make you examine your understanding of heaven and hell. "You Want It Made out of What?" will challenge you to wonder when you have made a god out of the gift instead of the Giver. "Can This Be Home?" will have you wondering about the exiles in your midst. And "The Night *They* Were There" will have you thinking about those you would be most comfortable — and uncomfortable — eating with.

THE TOPSY–TURVY KINGDOM:
More Stories for Your Faith Journey
by James L. Henderschedt
Paperbound $7.95, 122 pages, 5 ½" x 8 ½"
ISBN 0-89390-177-6

Twenty-one stories of faith that turn the ordinary into the extraordinary. Find out why Carmen is glad she has to work on Thanksgiving Day, what happens when a busy man goes to a peace rally, and who was the greatest advance man any show ever had. In these stories bullies learn manners, workaholics find their way home, and young lawyers learn to use discernment with their clients. Through them all, the spiritual pilgrim will find deep, thought-provoking ideas. Use them for preaching, for religious education, or just for your own enjoyment.

THE MAGIC STONE
And Other Stories for the Faith Journey
by James L. Henderschedt
Paperbound $7.95, 95 pages, 5 ½" x 8 ½"
ISBN 0-89390-116-4

The eternal wisdom of Scripture comes alive in the everyday setting of modern life in The Magic Stone. Read this book for enrichment, share the stories with others — your congregation, adult education class, or prayer group — and watch the word come to life for them. These inspirational stories are filled with touches of humor and suspense. Delightful, amazing, and most of all thought provoking, the reader or the listener will reflect on the real meaning behind the story and its spiritual significance for their own lives.

FORGIVE: Stories of Reconciliation
by Lou Ruoff
Paperbound, $8.95, 102 pages, 5 ½" x 8 ½"
ISBN 0-89390-198-9

In falling autumn leaves, Lou Ruoff sees the power of fallen humans to heal themselves and others; in the tears of a little girl he sees the hope that Judas lacked; in a simple request for eye glasses he sees the answer to humanity's distorted vision. The author combines stories from the Bible with his own experience of hurt, rejection, discrimination, and anger. In the power and simplicity of his stories, Ruoff draws the reader to trust in God's love to forgive and be forgiven. The message of these stories will stay with you for a long time.

NO KIDDING, GOD, WHERE ARE YOU?
Parables of Ordinary Experience
by Lou Ruoff
Paperbound, $7.95 100 pages, 5 ½" x 8 ½"
ISBN 0-89390-141-5

Feeling alone? Abandoned by God? Read these extraordinary stories of the ordinary and the Gospel message will come alive to you in a new and deeper way. Lou Ruoff, with his keen perception of the average person's pain, uses his wonderful storytelling gifts to apply the lessons in Jesus' parables to the commonplace happenings of modern life. Find the message in a smashed sand castle at the beach, and see the love of God in a game of hopscotch. This book is loaded with spiritual nourishment for everyone.

WINTER DREAMS and Other Such Friendly Dragons
by Joseph J. Juknialis
Paperbound $7.95, 87 pages, 6" x 9"
ISBN 0-89390-010-9

Delightful, gentle stories that transport the reader to a world of hope. In drama, fairytale, and fable the author fills us with stories of old and valued principles. If Winter prepares us for birth, dreams prepare us for what will be. In these fifteen stories, let yourself rejoice that you live in the season of Winter and you journey through the dreams of your spirit.

ANGELS TO WISH BY:
A Book of Story-Prayers
by Joseph J. Juknialis
Paperbound $7.95, 136 pages, 6" x 9"
ISBN 089390-051-6

These beautiful stories can be used in liturgical and paraliturgical celebrations. The book contains prayers, Scripture, reflections—all pointed to giving you a deeper insight into Christian faith and what that faith calls you to do. Read about the Bag Lady, Josh and the free wish, the Banjo man. Sing the songs that accompany some of the stories. This book is a wonderful aid for teachers, homilists, and catechists.

A STILLNESS WITHOUT SHADOWS
by Joseph J. Juknialis
Paperbound $7.95 75 pages, 6" x 9"
ISBN 0-89390-081-8

If you enjoyed Joseph Juknialis other books, you will love **A Stillness Without Shadows**. These new stories spell out the way faith can be lived — but sometimes isn't. Read "The Lady of the Grand," "The Cup," or "The Golden Dove" to reflect on the depth of God's love and the strength of human weakness. Included is an appendix that gives wonderful tips on how to use the stories in liturgies and class settings.

WHEN GOD BEGAN IN THE MIDDLE
by Joseph J. Juknialis
Paperback $7.95, 101 pages, 6" x 9"
ISBN 0-89390-027-3

Our God is a God who comes into the middle of everything. God comes into the middle of our sin, and we begin to know mercy. He comes into the middle of our loneliness, and we begin to be transformed into the image and likeness of love. God comes into the middle of death, and gives life. Read these fantasy stories and reflect on times in your own life when God began in the middle.

STORY AS A WAY TO GOD
A Guide for Storytellers
by H. Maxwell Butcher
Paperbound, $11.95 153 pages, 5 ½" x 8 ½"
ISBN: 0-89390-201-2

This book will open your eyes to find God's story everywhere. The message of God is hidden in our novels, movies, poems, and plays. The homilist, the teacher, and the counselor will learn how to improve their storytelling skills as they read Maxwell Butcher's careful analysis of story type from comedy and tragedy to melodrama and "resurrection literature." Tips include how to avoid a "too easy" ending, and why a story must "stretch" the reader. From **Sound of Music** to **Lord of the Rings** the author convinces you that telling a story is the best way to share the Christian message, and he challenges you to be open to ways that you, too, can tell God's story.

OTHER GOOD BOOKS
ABOUT STORIES AND STORYTELLING

STORYTELLING STEP BY STEP
by Marsh Cassady
Paperbound, $9.95, 156 pages, 5 ½" x 8 ½"
ISBN 0-89390-183-0

This handbook for storytellers breaks down the elements you need for successful storytelling. Find out about the relationship between the story and the teller. Learn how to adapt a story for a particular audience; how to choose a story that matches the occasion; and how to use voice, gesture and props to enhance your storytelling.

CREATING STORIES FOR STORYTELLING
by Marsh Cassady
Paperbound, $9.95 144 pages, 5 ½" x 8 ½"
ISBN 0-89390-205-5

Cassady continues to instruct his readers in the art of storytelling. Here he gives tips on how to get ideas for creating stories, how to develop a plot, create tension, and write dialogue that will hold your listener's attention.

TELLING STORIES LIKE JESUS DID
Creative Parables for Teachers
by Christelle L. Estrada
Paperbound $8.95, 100 pages, 5 ½" x 8 ½"
ISBN 0-89390-177-6

Christelle Estrada retells ten parables from Luke's Gospel. then reinterprets each message in terms today's children can understand. Teachers searching for a way to interpret the Gospel message of salvation for children will find this book an excellent guide.

BALLOONS! CANDY! TOYS!
And Other Parables for Storytellers
by Daryl Olszewski
Paperbound $8.95, 100 pages, 5 ½" x 8 ½"
ISBN 0-89390-069-9

Daryl Olszewski's prayerful interpretations of nine parables from Scripture catch at the heart of the reader. He begins by reflecting on some aspect of a Gospel story like the heart of stone. Then he tells the story through the perception of an inanimate object and finishes with a commentary that shows how to make stories into faith experience for children and adults. This is great for teachers, storytellers, and anyone who enjoys new reflections on ageless Gospel stories.

STORIES FOR CHILDREN

PARABLES FOR LITTLE PEOPLE
by Lawrence Castagnola, S.J.
Paperbound $7.95, 101 pages, 5 ½" x 8 ½"
ISBN 0-89390-034-6

Sweet, humorous stories that teach children basic values. They will learn about race relations through "The Rainbow People," and overcoming self-pity through "Arnold the Elephant." Children will love these stories and ask for more, and teachers, catechists, and parents will delight in teaching children through these sixteen mighty little parables.

MORE PARABLES FOR LITTLE PEOPLE
by Larry Castagnola, S.J.
Paperbound 100 pages, 5 ½" x 8 ½"
ISBN 0-89390-095-8

This sequel to **Parables for Little People** has 15 more charming children's stories with happy, positive messages. Seven of the new stories teach the Gospel themes of sharing, caring, non-violence, and human rights. The rest retell the Gospel stories without naming the original characters. This is a great book for children, teachers, and parents.

ORDER FORM

Order from your local bookstore, or mail this form to:

QTY TITLE   PRICE   TOTAL

_____
_____
_____
_____

Subtotal:_____
CA residents add 7¼% sales tax:_____
(Santa Clara Co. add 8¼% sales tax)
Postage and handling:_____
($2 for orders up to $20,
10% of order over $20
but less than $150,
$15 for order of $150 or more.)
Total amount:_____

Resource Publications, Inc.
160 E. Virginia St., Suite 290
San Jose, CA 95112-5876
or call (408) 286-8505.

☐ My check or money order is enclosed.

☐ Charge my ☐ VISA ☐ MC. Expires:_____

Card#_____-_____-_____-_____

Signature:_____

Name: _____

Institution:_____

Street: _____

City/St/Zip:_____

AZ